Joe Bennett was born in Eastbou... variety of countries. He now writes just outside Christchurch, New Ze... Columnist of the Year at the Qantas ...or the third time in six years.

Praise from New Zealand for Joe Bennett's journalism:

'Joe Bennett can take the ordinary and make it magical in a few crisp sentences'
Dunedin Star

'Joe Bennett is a man who can construct two sentences so that you become desperate to read the third'
The Press (Christchurch)

'Bennett is a national treasure'
Southland Times

'Joe Bennett achieves the most difficult kind of writing – the kind that looks effortless'
New Zealand Listener

'Bennett's writing is a splendid example of how simple English can be employed to devastating effect. He makes our other columnists seem earnest, stolid and verbose'
North & South

Also by Joe Bennett

Bedside Goats and Other Lovers

Fun Run and Other Oxymorons

A Land of Two Halves

Mustn't Grumble

Love, Death, Washing-Up, Etc.

Joe Bennett

POCKET
BOOKS

LONDON • SYDNEY • NEW YORK • TORONTO

First published in Great Britain by Pocket Books in 2007
An imprint of Simon & Schuster UK Ltd
A CBS COMPANY

The articles in this book have previously been published in
New Zealand in five books: *Doggone* (2002), *Barking* (2003),
Unmuzzled (2004), *Dogmatic* (2005) and *Down Boy* (2006),
all published by Hazard Press. The articles first appeared in
New Zealand in *The Press* (Christchurch), *Evening Post*, *New
Zealand Herald*, *Hawke's Bay Today*, *Otago Daily Times*,
Dominion Post (Wellington), *Waikato Daily Times*, *Southland
Times* or the *New Zealand Gardener*.

1 3 5 7 9 10 8 6 4 2

Simon & Schuster UK Ltd
Africa House
64–78 Kingsway
London WC2B 6AH

www.simonsays.co.uk

Simon & Schuster Australia
Sydney

ISBN: 978-1-84739-108-7

Typeset in Granjon by M Rules
Printed and bound in Great Britain by
Cox & Wyman Ltd, Reading, Berks

to Albert Arriola and to hope

Contents

Preface   xi

I shall   1
The cricket, exclamation mark   4
Cuchulain's children   7
White rectangular domestic things   10
Like solitary sex   13
The end of the soap   16
Permanent, fixed and safe   19
Several worsts   23
Natch   26
Eyes right   29
He's in a meeting   32
I wish they didn't   35
Be luggage   38
Seven minutes to live   41
He was a pretty good dog   44
Lotsadeadredindians   47
Big cherub   51

Land you can play with   54

Dreams on wheels   57

All squared away   60

At two drunks swimming   63

Girlie sox   66

Oi Popey-boy   69

Shock revelations   73

Ooooh la bloody la   76

Wrong room   80

Hope is dead   83

No children litter the step   87

Hot wet air   90

Easter rising   94

How to be happy   97

Lucy mon   100

At the Dickens   103

Playing with god   107

Warm, wet and threatless   111

Lies to spare   114

A betting man   118

Night-time angels   122

Hello, heat   125

Probe and rectify, please   128

McFilm   132

Arachnametaphor   136

Dinnerhoea   139

Ridiculously excited   142

Necks, please   145

Stuff love   149

Where do you go to? 152

Ballooooooon 155

Glossy lala 158

Grammar with teeth 161

Pap 164

Weather or not 168

Gumdigger 172

Consider the zip 176

Dead snapper 179

I, speechwriter 183

DNAisy 187

Let's boulder 191

Dear College of Cardinals 195

Entropic cookery 199

Keep 'em poor 203

Fifty thousand an hour, money-makingly 207

A short stack with Ben 211

Light thickens with dogs 215

For we are young and free 219

See me saw 223

Not if, but when 226

Joe, you're an angel 231

Funny and true 234

Dead classy 238

Pam's pups 241

Reverend reasoning 245

One 249

Hitch 253

Welcome 257

Flies say no   260

The threshold of the ginge   263

Rod and gut   266

Speak to us   269

I want some of that   272

On making a bed   275

Mister Muster   279

The grid of seduction   283

Up Apophthegm Mountain   286

Preface

Writing is the only way I know how to think. If I don't write as I go, thoughts wander miles from where they started. And then I forget where they started.

I find most things easier than thinking. And belief, in particular, is easier than thinking. Everything around us urges us to believe – to believe in Manchester United, under-arm deodorant, God, package holidays, love, health food, superannuation funds, educational theory, the news, disinfectant, tomorrow, lotteries, liposuction, the ubiquity of paedophiles, presidents. I find that when I think about these things, I generally end up laughing.

These pieces were written between 2000 and 2006. I have resisted the urge to change what I wrote in order to look wise before the event. I make no claim to prophecy. I've never been good at prediction. In 1998 a certain terrorist first swam into the public consciousness. I dubbed him Something Bin Something. 'A year from now,' I wrote, 'his name will mean nothing.' I've always been rather proud of that.

Joe Bennett
Lyttelton, New Zealand, May 2007

I shall

Yes of course I've made a New Year's resolution. I shall behave better at parties.

When I am going to a party in 2002 I shall not take the bottle of Fijian riesling that someone once brought to my party because someone once brought it to their party. And when I take the Fijian riesling I shall not carry it in with my hand over the label, nor shall I go straight to the kitchen and hide it among the other bottles of Fijian riesling and look in the fridge for beer.

I shall not pretend to recognise people. When someone at a party says, 'Hello Joe, how lovely to see you again', I shall not say it is lovely to see them again. I shall say, 'What's your name?'

When people tell me their name I shall use it five times in the first five sentences so as not to forget it. When I forget it I shall not substitute the word 'mate'

When I kiss a woman at a party I shall not let the woman dictate how we are going to kiss. I shall decide for myself whether it is to be the lips, the cheek or the full facial bypass. If it is the full facial bypass I shall not nibble the ear. If it is the lips I shall wait a full minute before wiping my mouth. When a man makes to hug me I shall go away.

If a conversation is boring I shall not say that I am just going to fetch a drink and then not come back. I shall say I am just going to the loo and then not come back. If I say I am just going to fetch a drink the bore can ask me to fetch him one too and we are back where we started.

I shall not escape bores by pretending to catch sight of someone I know on the far side of the room and saying, 'Excuse me a minute.' Nor shall I beckon a friend across, introduce the friend to the bore and then go away.

If a friend beckons me across to meet someone I shall go away. I shall go to the back doorstep to smoke and play with the dog.

I shall not spend long periods at parties sitting on the back doorstep smoking and playing with the dog. Nor shall I steal chicken vol-au-vents to feed the dog with. Nor shall I give it sips of Fijian riesling.

I shall always take a warm sweater to parties because it can get cold on the back door step. A cushion would be a good idea too. And some chicken vol-au-vents.

When the party begins at 8 o'clock I shall not go to the pub first for just a quick one. Nor shall I stay at home with a book until it is too late to go to the party and then ring up in the morning and say I've just looked in the diary and how sorry I am to have missed it and was it fun and we must do it again soon.

I shall never say we must do it again soon.

When someone at a party tells me something private and juicy I shall not tell it to the next person I talk to without first asking them if they can keep a secret. If they say no I shall not just go ahead and tell them anyway.

When people ask me if I can keep a secret I shall say no. They will just go ahead and tell me anyway.

I shall not stay right to the end of parties. When I stay right to the end of parties I shall not boast that I used to be reasonably good at gymnastics. When I boast that I used to be reasonably good at gymnastics I shall not offer to do a handstand. I shall always choose a well-carpeted bit of the house to do the handstand in.

When people at parties ask me if I'd be willing to help out with the bring-and-buy sale for the local kindergarten I shall say no. And when they ring up the next day to ask if I really meant it when I said yes, I shall not say, 'Of course I meant it.' I shall say, 'No, I didn't mean it.'

When they tell me the date of the bring-and-buy sale I shall not say, 'What a pity. I'll be out of town that day.' Nor shall I then go out of town that day in case someone rings from the bring-and-buy sale.

When the beer runs out at parties I shall not drink from left-over cans that are half full. I shall sieve them first to get the cigarette ends out.

I shall not dance.

The cricket, exclamation mark

'Sorry but no,' I said into the receiver. 'It's kind of you and I'd really like to go. I just love Bulgarian films, especially from the 50s, those gritty black and white tonal values, that daring absence of plot, but it's just . . .'

'You want to watch the cricket,' she said.

'The cricket,' I said with vehemence, 'the cricket, exclamation mark. Yes I do.'

'Cricket,' she said in the manner of a public health official diagnosing threadwarts, 'is 20 boys who somehow got through puberty but didn't let it change a thing, wasting five days of what they like to think of as their lives playing a game devised in the nineteenth century to keep schoolboys from masturbating and the British Empire from revolting, a game that, if it ever had any virtue, has now surrendered it entirely to commercial interests.'

'Twenty-two boys,' I said.

'Haven't you noticed,' she swept on, 'that the team from this country is sponsored by an offshore telecommunications company and that the team from the other country is sponsored by another offshore telecommunications company and that the whole shebang is televised by a third offshore telecommunications company whose only purpose is to keep drongos like you rooted to the sofa, beer in hand and brain in neutral, cramming pepperoni pizzas into your mouth for 50 years until you die? You're a dupe, a stooge, a dummy, a victim of commercial manipulation, a life-form in suspension, a passive receptacle for trash, a donkey at the water wheel drawn ever forward by the synthetic allure of the business of sport. It's manhood by proxy, war by proxy, nationalism by proxy.' She paused for breath.

'I wish,' I said, 'you wouldn't say offshore. What's wrong with foreign? Or,' I added conciliatorily, 'even overseas', but she was in no mood for conciliation.

'The saddest thing of all,' she said, and the word 'said' comes nowhere near accommodating the rising swell of her passion, 'are the people known as commentators, aged fools who once upon a time were young and played the game until their bodies betrayed them and who were then so deeply terrified of having to grow up that they scuttled like so many shell-less hermit crabs into the commentary box where they could bathe forever in the perpetual infancy of reminiscence and mendacity.'

'I see,' I said.

'Is that all,' she snorted, 'all you've got to say to defend the way you choose to spend a day of your life?'

'It ought to be,' I said, 'but since you ask, it isn't. Cricket's beautiful.'

Her gasp was gratifying.

'Truly beautiful,' I said. 'Like you,' I almost added, before wisdom stilled my tongue. 'Have you not,' I asked, 'seen Shane Warne? A man whose manner I find utterly repellent, a man who has the aura of a moral vacuum, a man whom I would cross the road to miss, but a man who bowls a cricket ball as Leonardo wielded paint. To watch him shuffle with his surfboy hair a few short strides towards the stumps, his wrist furled up, his fingers wrapped like tentacles around the ball and then to toss a leg break up in such a way that it will dip and curve and land and bite and spit and leave a batsman baffled, that, my dear, is beauty. Forget the artist – Leonardo, after all, had pimples and breath like Agent Orange – but love the art.

'And have you not,' I added, 'seen Stephen Fleming bat? He gropes and looks ungainly and then from furnaces where art is forged he leans onto a bent front knee and puts the ball past extra cover so sweetly that confectioners swoon. The right elbow may not be elevated as the coaching books would wish but that's the imperfection that makes beauty. There are moments when he conjures up a hint of David Gower, and praise can go no higher. Gower batted like the Holy Ghost in whites.

'I could go on,' I said. 'I could tell you of a dumpy little Englishman called Philip Sharpe who caught the ball at slip with such deft ease I swear that, had he wished, he could have plucked a swallow from the summer air.

'And even,' I continued, 'in these grim commercial times of sponsorship and chewing gum, the sport can still produce a game like the one that has just been, a game that over five long days swung one way then the other, a game embracing luck and misery along the way, and heroism, courage, subtlety and thought, a game of such intensity it drained the colour from my hair. And in the end it was a draw. Beat that for irony,' I said. 'Beat that for simulation of the way we are. Beat that.'

She couldn't. She'd gone.

Cuchulain's children

No, no, it just won't do, this Irish stuff. It's got to stop.

Now I'm as fond of a pint of stout as the next man, so come St Patrick's Day the next man and I duly toddled down to the joke local Irish bar where the heirs to the warrior tradition of Cuchulain the Strong were wearing wigs of green tinsel. But at least they'd maintained the ancient Irish tradition of emigrating.

So many Paddies have hightailed it out of Ireland that only the Catholic church's sexual ethics have kept the place populated. Not that there's anything wrong with emigrating. I've done a fair swag of it myself but if you ever catch me boohooing for the land of my birth, kindly take a shillelagh to my softer parts then lash me to the mizzen of the first ship home.

The Irish have made boohooing into an art. Apart from people, their only export crop is nostalgia, as summed up by the character in a Hardy novel who 'sang sweet songs of his own dear country that he loved so much as never to have revisited it'. Because, of course, no sooner is Paddy O'Flaherty on the boat bound for Opportunity than he's humming 'Danny Boy', going misty-eyed at any mention of the Emerald Isle and acquiring a rackful of CDs by Daniel O'Bleeding Donnell.

Most of the Irish have emigrated for that most cogent of reasons, poverty. Too few spuds on the table for a family of 27 meant Liam took the first boat to New York where his love of fighting after the pub shut would lead him naturally into the police force. Once there he could start lying.

Liam and his mates the world over have woven not so much a tissue of lies about poor old Ireland as a heavy-duty tarpaulin. And it's a tarpaulin that the rest of the world, in the manner of a snake ingesting a goat, has swallowed.

Bung the word Irish in front of anything these days and it sells. Irish ballads, Irish tenors, and, most wonderful of all, traditional Irish dancing featuring a man in traditional sequined trousers and a line up of colleens in apt but invisible straitjackets, all of them heel-and-toeing it as if picking their way through an IRA bomb stash. The whole shebang is as authentically Irish as coq au vin.

Heritage, they call it, of a piece with the rich Irish literary tradition starring Jonathan Swift who spent three-quarters of his life in London, James Joyce who set up shop in either Paris or Zurich – I can't remember and don't care which, and neither did he, so long as it wasn't Dublin – and dreary Sam Beckett who did most of his waiting for O'Godot on the left bank of the Seine. Most recently we've had Frank McCourt. Son of a stout-sodden ne'er-do-well who spectacularly failed to keep his family of 50 in bread and pigsheads, dear old Frank headed across the Atlantic with understandable haste to write an account of his childhood with such lyrical intensity that every author envies him his deprivation. His tumbledown place of birth has become a shrine for semi-literate female tourists who've fallen in love with the heaving of Michael Flatley's chest or Val Doonican's cable-knit cardigan.

And then there are the Irish pubs. Oh spare us. To qualify as an Irish pub you've got to serve Guinness and play an over-loud CD of fiddle music. That's it. Plus a dozen green balloons on March 17th and a sturdy bag for lugging the loot to the bank. Irish pubs have sprung up wherever market research has revealed an untapped seam of bogus sentiment. That means everywhere. A former pupil of mine who's as Irish as a mob of hoggets has recently opened one in São Paulo. Hong Kong's got them like measles. The only place that hasn't got Irish pubs as the world knows them is Ireland.

I've been to Ireland. It's wet. The typical pub holds a wall-eyed son of the soil called Pete gobbing gloomily into a fire of the same name and wondering why he didn't join Dominic, Moirag et al on the first boat to Elsewhere, while the raddled barmaid breaks occasionally into a basso profundo rendition of 'One Day at a Time, Sweet Jesus' in the hope of sucking in a tourist. Meanwhile round the back of this scene of Irish authenticity lurks a bulldozer with the engine running on Euro tax dollars just waiting for the nod from Brussels to bowl the wreck of a pub and put up a tilt slab factory to assemble a thousand televisions a day so the tourist board can continue to beam images of old Ireland to every expatriate Paddy in the globe.

If you imagine we live in a secular age, freed from the superstitious burden of myth, just think Ireland.

White rectangular domestic things

Glory be to God for dappled things, said Gerard Manley Hopkins, going on to sing a hymn of praise to feathers on a thrush's chest and speckles on a trout. And that's just fine by me. I like those things a lot, or quite a lot, or somewhat anyway. But though I'm happy for the thrush and trout, as far as I'm concerned it's glory be to God for white rectangular domestic things. You know the things I mean, the tomb-like metal boxes coated in enamel by a process I can only guess at, the boxes that stand mute and patient round the house, the things we notice only when they go kaput and then because they very rarely do. I mean the washing machine. I mean the stove and tumble drier, and, most glorious of all the glories owing unto Him on high, the fridge. They also serve who only stand and hum.

The fridge is loyal and steadfast as a dog that doesn't need to go for walks – although admittedly in one of Owen Marshall's lovely stories there's a fridge that wanders through a farmhouse kitchen, driven by its lurching motor, cubical and android and tethered by a leash of brown electric cable, but even then it's not a threat to flesh, just idiosyncratically quaint.

My own fridge never wanders. For fifteen years I've fed it with a tiny quantity of lifeblood from the national grid and in exchange it's kept its faith with me. It may have come, I don't recall, with densely worded guarantees protecting me from shoddy workmanship, but if it did that guarantee has long since disappeared and rotted in some unremembered place, and all the while the fridge has chuntered on, a self-containing cube of chilliness, a geographic region in itself, distinct and unaffected by the vagaries of weather in the world beyond. Somehow, unlike the other stuff about the house, it doesn't seem to gather dirt. For though I never run a cleaning cloth about its walls, it stands amid the squalor like a virgin in a brothel.

For sure appalling crud collects beneath it, stuff that's greasy brown and sticky, stuff that takes a day of scrubbing with a brush to shift – or 30 seconds licking from a dog – but to blame the fridge for that would be to lay the blame on Downing Street for sheltering Tony Blair.

It's got no catch upon its door. I don't know how it does it but it opens with the application of a feather touch and it closes with a gentleness that couldn't hurt the fingers of the frailest child, and yet when closed it's sealed as surely as a sleeping eye. Not even that most daring of adventurers, the ant, can pierce the fridge's seal. The ant that undissuadably infests all places that it shouldn't, the ant whose six incessant legs will one day tread the earth in meek supremacy, the ant that feasts on scraps and dust and eyes of corpses, the ant that seeps through cracks as thin as hairs, the ant that dies unmourned in millions devoted to its species' greater good, the ant that can move boulders from its path and men to tears, can't penetrate my fridge's silent gentle seal.

A fridge is testament to men. By men I don't mean man in general, I mean men, specific men with names and families, men who over the long centuries have fathomed how to wrest a metal out of rock, who've somehow found the way to manufacture plastic, who've buried taps in trees and sauntered from the forest with a cup of rubber, who've harnessed electricity from lakes, who've played with brains and fingers to construct a motor that just goes on going on.

Yet I, though born and raised in the most technical of centuries, am capable of none of these extraordinary things. I take them as my due for being me. I sip the sweat that poured from others' brows and never give my deep dependency a second thought, reserving for myself the right to pout and sulk and squeal that I'm hard done by, that I fall upon the thorns of life and bleed, without acknowledging that I am blessed with ease and plenty and a fridge.

Why, even 50 years ago a fridge was rare as honesty. In those days milk went off and butter melted, a fish in summer lasted only hours and salmonella flourished. If summer food was to be tasted in the winter it had to be preserved and rendered sour with vinegar or salt, or boiled or pickled, dried or cured or sealed in great preserving jars like surgeon's specimens. Those ancient arts no longer matter much. The fridge has done them down.

So Gerard Manley Hopkins, Jesuit and poet, glory be to God for thrush and trout indeed, but I beg leave to add the fridge is cool.

Like solitary sex

The noisy electrician has been going to the gym for six months now. His Achilles tendon went ping last year and he says he goes to the gym to strengthen it. But really he goes there because he's a runty weed. He's had more sand in his face than a Bedouin.

He has often urged me to join him. I have resisted, partly because all my Achilles tendons are in the pink, but mainly because I am not a runty weed. My mother used to boast that I was sturdy. And once a shop assistant told me I was well-built. I was trying on a pair of jeans at the time and they had got stuck at my thighs.

But the electrician is an insistent man and yesterday I joined him. The gym carpark was loud with music. Through a second-floor window I could see the top halves of people doing aerobics. Incredibly some of them seemed to be men. I was impressed by the electrician's speed and strength as he stopped me getting back into my car.

At reception I had to sign a form that said it wouldn't be the gym's fault if I died. I also had to give a list of my goals. When I said I didn't have any goals the receptionist said I had to, so I wrote 'happiness'. She looked at me.

At the bottom of the form was a diagram of the human body for me to circle the places where I had suffered injuries. I found that if I went back far enough I could circle everything except my crotch. Then I remembered a childhood zip and circled the lot.

The gym was crammed with the sort of home-exercise machines you see advertised on television by women with leotards and teeth. But these machines were different from the ones in people's houses in that they were being used.

Some of the machines had little holders on them. I was the only person there not carrying a baby's bottle full of water.

By way of a warm-up the electrician and I rode bicycles to nowhere. A screen on the handlebars told me the calories I had expended and the kilometres I hadn't travelled. It didn't tell me the degree to which the saddle was chafing my thighs. Nor did it need to.

The woman on the next bike was reading a magazine. I leaned across to read about Prince Harry and discovered some good drinking tips.

After ten minutes I was very warmed up. When the electrician asked me how I was feeling I didn't bother to reply. A visual scan revealed that the thigh-chafing quotient was 93 per cent.

The people in the gym fell into two categories. There were those with good bodies and those with less good bodies. Those with good bodies wore dinky little shorts and singlets. Those with less good bodies wore baggy shorts and T-shirts.

Some of the people with good bodies walked around a lot but didn't seem to take much exercise. Those with less good bodies worked hard all the time.

There were several large mirrors whose athletic purpose wasn't immediately apparent. One man with thighs like half-g's and biceps like medicine balls held dumb-bells in front of a mirror. Every ten seconds or so he knelt before his reflection.

Few people spoke. Even fewer smiled. Some stole glances at what others were doing, but most wore looks of anguish or of self-absorption. We gym bunnies look as if we are engaged in solitary sex. Personal trainers were on patrol, distinguishable by their good bodies, rather less good uniforms and enormous sports shoes full of technology.

My arms have always been strong. On the bench press machine the runty electrician did twelve repetitions and then let me have a go. I chose to stop at ten. Then he did twelve more and I did six. I would have done seven but he stopped me, out of concern for a blood vessel in my face. While he carried on I went to reception to borrow a baby's water bottle. The girl asked how I was feeling. 'Rubbery,' I said. 'That's nice,' she said.

We did more arm weights and leg weights and then we worked on our abs. We lay down and sat up. We crunched and we writhed like upturned tortoises. We groaned and we gasped – although the electrician had learnt to do so silently.

After an hour I said I thought I shouldn't overdo it on my first day. The electrician said he normally did two hours, but he showed me where the sauna was. I proved to be good at the sauna.

On the way out the cheerful girl asked me if I would like to join. I said I would think about it. I have thought about it. I lead a sedentary life and I think I should. I shall write them a cheque just as soon as I can move my arms.

The end of the soap

The Reaper's trying to put the wind up me but he's wasting his time. Everywhere I go I hear him sharpening his scythe with a noise like fingernails on a blackboard but I don't give a fig. What he doesn't understand is that I've got unfinished business. I mean to outlive my soap.

In 1992 the first XI at a school where I was teaching went to Australia to get beaten. They needed money to get there so the entrepreneurial daddy of the wicketkeeper bought them, as one does, a containerload of Indonesian soap. It was called GIV and it was the colour of dung. He sent the boys out to sell it by the box load. Each box held 48. I bought three boxes. That's a gross of soap cakes. Today, after nine years, I finished the first box.

The stuff's still as good as the day it was made – which isn't actually that good – but I intend to use it all. Call me mean, call me stubborn, but it's become a quiet obsession, an obsession that should please the dingbats who insist that the secret of life is goal-setting. There's something about the mute durability of this mass of GIV, the patience with which it merely squats in my cupboard and waits, that excites my competitive urge. I've got eighteen more years of GIV in my cupboard and I intend to take them.

But the Reaper insists in offering me warnings. Only today I went to visit an old friend who isn't old but is in hospital. Two days ago at work he developed hot flushes as if he'd just drunk five pints of Guinness in a sauna. Ten minutes later he was in the cardiac unit having a bottle scourer shoved up an artery in his thigh. Apparently a bit of something had dislodged from the wall of something else, jammed up against his ventricles and starved his heart of blood. If he hadn't been in close proximity to a hospitalful of gadgets he'd have been reaped.

As it was he was able to sit cheerfully up in bed while the white-coated ones went at his plumbing. Furthermore, and I envy him this bit, the whole exercise was played out on a wide-screen TV beside the bed and he was allowed to watch his own innards being painlessly reamed. All that was lacking, he said, were the slo-mos and the beer.

He's now condemned to a life of margarine but is otherwise hunky-dory and no more likely than you or I to suffer a recurrence. Apparently the medicos were just a little miffed during the post-op interrogation of his lifestyle to discover that he didn't smoke, jogged a lot and drank that hideous green milk. It seems the docs still believe in Sunday school notions of death being the wages of sin rather than the wages of living. They are wedded, the darlings, to the principle of cause and effect, which is all very well in the test-tube but a little less than precise in the big wide world of experience.

Anyway I got great vicarious excitement from someone else tap-tapping on death's door. We all know in theory about time's winged chariot but this chap had come nose to nose with its radiator grille. I drove home from the hospital with scythe-sharpening noises ringing in my skull, made a cup of coffee, checked the email and got another dose of the Grim One.

A friend in Germany had written to tell me she'd been flattened by a BMW. It left her prone and all unnoticed on the autobahn with the life dripping out of her. But then who should stroll along but her hairdresser, and he of the combs and curlers did the needful, stemming the blood, summoning the ambulance and insisting on holding her hand all the way to the hospital and then all through the night. She couldn't speak too highly of Herr Dresser. And, like my pal with the ticker, she is going to be fine. At the same time I couldn't help thinking that if my local barber, with his famously bloodstained apron, were to offer me such support when I was close to croaking, I doubt if I'd want to pull through.

So the evidence is clear that the Reaper's on the prowl in my vicinity, but he's whistling into the wind. I am measuring out my life in boxes of GIV and I am confident they'll see me through to indoor bowls and slippers. What's more I'm going to send a cake of GIV to each of my shaken friends. I shall tell them to use it slowly.

Permanent, fixed and safe

'I told him he was a fool,' said the journalist. I asked why.

'Because,' said the journalist, 'he threw in a perfectly good job – pension, promotion, security, the lot – threw it in and cashed up and . . .'

He paused while the waiter arrived with our lunch.

'And what?' I asked.

'And bought a second-hand bookshop. And not even a decent one. It's tucked up some side street visited only by dogs and old women.'

'Not much point in asking how he's doing then?'

'No,' said the journalist, 'there isn't', and he snorted, and we looked down at our plates. Mine held fish, his a steak in a blood puddle. He pinioned the steak with a fork and sawed at the corner. I watched the fibres tear and ooze.

It's not a rare dream, I think, to run a second-hand bookshop. To spend your more boisterous years wringing money from the world and then to shrink into a quiet street and spend the balance of days among tall walls of books.

The world is too much with us. Walls of books keep it off. Books are the world at one remove. They are permanent, fixed and safe. They can be beautiful but they can't hurt, not really hurt. The wounds inflicted by reading, the griefs and fears, are theatrical wounds, are pleasant pain.

To sit all day amid old books, while outside the traffic hisses through the wet winter, going somewhere, urgent and frantic. To see the occasional customer, a quiet soul in a drab raincoat who wanders along the spines of knowledge, cocking his head to catch the titles, his nature illustrated by the shelves he heads for.

It is not business, or rather it is as close to not being business as business can be. Most of the authors are dead and so are most of the books. The authors who are judged to be live currency will be taken from the shelves within days of coming in, but most will prove to be groats or guineas, no longer current in the busy spending minds that throng the city. A second-hand bookshop is a graveyard of spent passions, and the proprietor is the sexton.

I often visit such shops and I do so in just the same way as I duck into a church. It is a quiet place, a sanctuary. I like the smell and the peace and I like the books.

Today I bought for $5 the *Selected Poems of Thomas Hardy*. Hardy made plenty of money from his novels but after *Jude the Obscure* he gave up prose and for the last fifteen years of his life wrote only poetry. It was his way of retiring from the busy streets. He left the new book shop in the high street with its bright pile of best sellers and moved, as it were, to the backstreet and the second-hand shop that just gets by.

On the flyleaf of the book I bought, written in cheap blue ball-point:

Danny
Merry Christmas
Good luck up the Whataroa
Happy Reading
Lots of love
Jackie.

If that doesn't make your spine tingle we have different vertebrae.
I would like to know if Danny read Hardy up the Whataroa. For
some reason I doubt that he did. I doubt even that he took the book
with him. But if he did, and if he sat with it in the evening, alone,
looking out over the deserted valley, he might have found these lines:

William Dewy, Tranter Reuben, Father Ledlow late at plough,
Robert's kin, and John's, and Ned's,
And the Squire, and Lady Susan, lie in Mellstock churchyard now.

And in the churchyard of the poem the voices of the dead speak:

We've no wish to hear the tidings, how the people's fortunes shift;
What your daily doings are;
Who are wedded, born, divided; if your lives beat slow or swift.

Was there perhaps some similar sense of withdrawal from the
world that drove Danny up the Whataroa, without his Jackie? And
is it perhaps the same urge that drives hermits into caves, monks
into monasteries, and busy businessmen into the isolation of a shop
selling second-hand books?

The journalist laid down his knife and fork.

'I went to see the bloke the other day,' he said. 'In his shop.'

'How was he?' I asked.

The journalist mopped the blood from his plate with a piece of bread and popped it in his mouth. 'Happy,' he said.

Several worsts

The worst of it is that I shall be fined a fat sum of money. No, I lie. The worst of it is, well, let's start at the beginning.

A windy afternoon, fragile sunshine thin as cellophane, chilliness coming off the sea at 40 kph, perfect for keeping the sand-castle-building, shallows-paddling, shell-collecting kiddiwinks off the beach and leaving it free for me and the dogs and the sticks I shall throw them.

Into the car and off to the beach, stopping only to post a letter to a madwoman. Past the sewage ponds we drive where the wind whips up little brown waves, on the crests of which the sunshine splinters. Right at the roundabout, my three-legged dog barking out the window at the smell of the salt, then over the bridge in, would you believe it, Bridge Street, and stopping at the junction with Marine Parade. Look right, look left, look right again along a road as clear as conscience. Only a single ancient woman hunched against the wind with a sad bag of groceries. The littoral is empty and the whole beach will be ours.

Swing right onto the beach road, then drive 200 yards past the blockhouse surf club with its desolate carpark and the conifers all crabbed from the sand-laden winds, and pull over to park in the bay of rough grass, glancing as I do so, oh so properly, in the mirror. Lights. Lights flashing red and blue in the radiator grille of an otherwise unmarked car.

I get out of my car and so does the cop. The dogs are puzzled. I've no idea what I've done wrong and yet already round the base of my neck unwanted bubbles of schoolboy guiltiness, fear of authority and a sense of being in the wrong are going crawlabout as they've not done for years. And a sort of pricking lightness in my arms and palms. And a knowledge that I'm only a couple of words away from blushing. I hate myself for all of it.

He calls me 'sir'. I don't call him anything. Around his belt the usual uninteresting paraphernalia of enforcement. On his feet the regulation heavy soles. I am old enough to have taught him.

He has stopped me, he says, because I was speeding. I want to say he hasn't stopped me. Here was my destination. I had already arrived and safely. But I do not say that. I say, God help me, 'Sorry'

'Eighty k,' he says, 'in a 50k zone. That's a little bit excessive.'

Mentally I gesture to the carnage I haven't wrought in my whirlwind passage down that deserted road. I gesture to the absence of strewn bodies, of orphaned children, of stoved-in sides of houses. But I say nothing. I feel simple injustice, that I, who drive like a spinster, who, since I turned 30 and the hormones stopped their roaring, have had a driving licence spotless as a wimple, who hurt nobody and pay my taxes and uphold the laws I don't find inconvenient, am now having my details laboriously recorded in his stage-policeman's flip-top note book.

'We're having a blitz on speed this month,' he says.

The woman with groceries battles past on the pavement, turning her hunch and her headscarf to look at me, pleased to see me caught. Trouble's good to watch.

'A blitz, a blitz on speed, oh that's just dandy. But not on speed like mine. My speed's okay. The speed you want is hoonish speed, the needless growling adolescent speed of nasty low-slung cars with spoiler-things, the speed of boys and men with horrid haircuts who go fast only to go fast, who speed in just the manner that a rooster crows. That's the speed you should be after, not middle-aged speed in a dirty old car on a poker-straight road with nothing to hit.'

Of course I don't say any of that. Instead, and to my deep astonishment, as if I were the sudden victim of ventriloquism, I hear myself say 'Thank you'. My tone of voice reminds me of a schoolboy in some ancient institution who stands after a caning and shakes his assailant's hand.

The cop drives away. I release the dogs, follow to the beach and kick the sand. The monstrous fine will be nasty but it's not what makes me kick. What swings that kick is petulance, a feeble whine of 'that's unfair', a deep conviction that the rules should not apply to me.

And also, more importantly, the glimpse I've just been granted of the schoolboy I had never much admired, extant still within my ageing frame, as craven, base and whining as he ever was. That's the worst of it.

Natch

Take several gallons of water and dump some sodium laureth sulphate into it, along with cocamidopropyl betaine, propylene glycol, butylene glycol, and a liberal slug of ethoxydiglycol. Add other polysyllables to taste and sprinkle with sodium chloride. Mix, heat, stir and cool, then bottle the result. What you've got is a lot of shampoo.

But before you stick it in boxes and pack it off to supermarkets in the hope that the unwashed millions will make you rich by hauling it from the shelves, you first must christen the stuff. And as you dunk it in the font, what name will you intone over its chemical complexity? Exactly. Got it in one. You'll call it 'Naturals'.

And so would I. And so, more importantly, did the nice people at Colgate Palmolive. They called their shampoo Naturals, and I've just bought a bottle of it and read the list of ingredients.

But before the Colgate Palmolive legal team come rumbling over the horizon waving writs, eager to prove in a court of law that all the ingredients of Naturals shampoo are indeed natural, I am happy to admit they may be right. I am willing to believe that somewhere in Thailand – which is where, by the way, they make their shampoo, for reasons of pure philanthropy and without thought to cheap labour – there are limpid pools of ethoxydiglycol to which the antelope come down shyly of an evening to bathe and sip.

I am willing to believe it because nature abounds in chemicals. Indeed nature is chemicals. Even as I am writing this, the ghost of fifth form chemistry has whispered in my innocent ear that sodium chloride is nothing more nor less than table salt, a substance as natural as malice. Quite what salt is doing in shampoo I've no idea, but neither do I care. The stuff seems to clean my hair all right. No, I have no beef with Colgate Palmolive. My beef is with the word natural.

Natural. Everybody loves natural. It seems like the word next door. A pretty thing with vowels in all the right places and well-proportioned consonants, but also a word so deeply wholesome that you would happily hire it to baby-sit.

But you would be wrong. Natural's a slut. It's the loose woman of the lexicon. Take a tour through the backstreets of the dictionary and you won't find a harder-working whore. In the world of advertising there's barely an executive who hasn't made use of little Miss Natural, who hasn't in some dank alley hugged her flexibility to his black and greedy heart.

Advertising executives love to lie with her because natural has become a synonym for good. Natural means grass and trees and sky and sunshine, gentle birds and quivering delicate antelope. But what we seem to have forgotten is that natural also means bubonic plague. Natural means leprosy and scorpions. Natural means death, drought and prunes.

The opposite of natural is unnatural, by which we mean man-made. And herein lies an oddity. We've come to think that man-made stuff is bad stuff. We couldn't be more wrong.

As Thomas Hobbes famously observed, and as I have never tired of repeating, the life of man used to be nasty, brutish and short. What made it so was nature. Today, by and large, our lives are pleasant, civil and long. And what has made them so is man. Nature gave us smallpox. Man wiped it out. Nature gave us tooth decay and man has given us dentists. Dentists are unnatural.

We have not always been foolish enough to believe that nature is purely nice. It was only in the early nineteenth century that people began to cherish the untouched bits of the world. Drips liked Shelley wrote odes to the west wind while everyone else took shelter from it. Wordsworth went into raptures over daffodils but had less to say about poison ivy. What they both needed was a week in the mountains in nothing but their underpants. And so do we.

Because then perhaps we might see through the nonsense. When we saw shampoo, or a tub of margarine or an underlay of magnets advertised as natural, we would scoff. The word has slept around too much. It has lost all meaning. It has become merely a nice noise.

Quite why this should have happened I can't tell you. I could hypothesise about the myth of Eden. I could speculate on collective guilt or on the ignorance of urban man. But I think I'll just go and rub salt in my hair.

Eyes right

The button that holds my trousers up came off so I went to the optician.

The trousers in question are my default trousers, in other words the trousers I put on when I don't think about what trousers I am putting on. Made from corduroy the colour of algae they are so moulded to my shape that at night I don't so much take them off as step out of them and leave them standing on the bedroom floor like a pair of Siamese sentries. In the morning I just step back into them and let them walk me to the coffee machine.

I don't blame my tailor for the lost button – I have had nothing but the best from Mr Hallenstein – instead I blame that thief of all things, time. Time has sucked my mighty shoulders south. If he keeps it up, by the year 2030 I'll look like the Pyramid of Cheops.

When I went to sew the button back on I found that time had also shrunk my arms. I could no longer hold a needle and thread far enough away for me to focus. I tried to pass a blur through a blur.

Once or twice I succeeded but I discovered my success only at the precise moment when I was parting my fingers to have another go and a fraction of a millisecond too late I felt the tiny resistance of the thread pulling through the eye of the needle like either a rich man or a camel. On the one occasion I did manage to stop with the needle threaded, requiring me only to seize the short end and pull it through, I seized the long end.

I could of course have used a magnifying glass but a magnifying glass needs holding and I was already holding the thread, the needle and my breath.

Do you know the difference between an optician, a dispensing optician, an optometrist and an ophthalmologist? Nor do I, but they are all like trap-door spiders. The phonebook revealed that there were thousands of them out there, all previously unnoticed by me, waiting with the patience of time itself for the inevitable day that would bring me and my wallet stumbling into their den. I chose the optician who printed his phone number in 36-point type on the grounds that he seemed like a man who knew his market.

There is pleasure in submitting to expertise, in handing your problem over to a man who knows. My optician was charming, patient and ridiculously young. He reassured me that the eye-test wouldn't hurt. I hadn't expected it to hurt. Now I did. But it didn't. He swung lights around, presented me with charts and diagrams, fixed an extraordinary machine in front of my face and peered deep into my eyes in the way that lovers are meant to but in my experience don't unless they're psychotic or dogs.

And having tested all that my eyes could do he popped onto the bridge of my nose a pair of slotted lensless spectacles that looked as though they had been forged by a neolithic blacksmith and into one of the slots he dropped a lens and asked if that was any better and I said it was worse and he said good, and then he dropped another lens in front of it and then another and then another and suddenly all was as clear and bright as the first morning of spring, and in the manner of a man who had just performed a conjuring trick he asked if that was better now and I said yes it was and I was most impressed but I had been hoping for a horn-rimmed pair.

With the aid of a cross-section diagram of an eye, a diagram similar to one that I remembered copying into a school exercise book in the early 1970s and labelling vitreous humour, aqueous humour, retina, iris and Dave Collier's a Prat, he explained that the lens in my eye was ageing. A baby can focus apparently on the tip of its nose – and from my limited acquaintance with babies it seems that most of them do – but gradually the eye stiffens and the focal length extends and forces us ultimately into the optician's lair.

The optician and I agreed that I could probably go a little while longer without glasses but we both knew as we said goodbye that it was really au revoir. He and time have got me on a thread and they can and will soon wind me in.

'Oh and by the way,' he said, as I went to close the door behind me.

'Yes?'

'Pull your trousers up.'

He's in a meeting

Whenever I ring a friend at a place of work and I am told that he or she is in a meeting I suspect that I am being lied to. Furthermore I hope that I am being lied to. I would not wish meetings on my friends.

The least nasty kind of meeting is the large-group kind. You can always rely on a loudmouth to hijack such a meeting. This allows everyone else to doodle at the back. The loudmouth wants to ride his hobbyhorse, a matter of great concern to the loudmouth but of none to anyone else. It is the chairman's job to push him off that hobbyhorse. The loudmouth is reluctant to be pushed off and the friction can be fun to watch. When the meeting is adjourned the agenda will be half completed and the loudmouth fully enraged.

A common feature of large-group meetings is the procedure expert. He is always a he and often bearded. He delights in seconding motions, insisting that people speak through the chair, and saying 'Point of order, Madam Chairperson'. He has no other contribution to make.

Large-group meetings become worse when they are divided into small-group meetings. Sometimes an amusingly overpaid facilitator is employed to facilitate this. With great skill he facilitates the gathering into little groups who each have a subject to 'brainstorm'. Brainstorm means to come up with ideas. The vogue for brainstorming stems from the belief that there is no such thing as a dumb idea. As it happens there are millions of dumb ideas. They are deemed worthy of attention only in brainstorming sessions. The group's scribe summarises the dumb ideas with a primary-coloured felt-tip marker on a remarkably large piece of paper.

Then all the little groups are facilitated back together into a large group for what is excitingly known as a plenary session. This is the only extant use of the word plenary. Plenary derives from the Latin plenus meaning full, but plenary sessions are rarely full because during the tea-break several people have snuck off. At the plenary session the scribe for each of the small groups displays the remarkably large piece of paper and speaks to the ideas on it. Meeting experts say 'speaks to the ideas' because only the ideas are listening.

When all the ideas have been spoken to, the facilitator summarises the meeting and sends a security company to collect his fee. Then someone on a lower salary collects all the remarkably large pieces of paper and stores them in a cupboard for future reference. Future reference means finding them five years later and throwing them away.

But most meetings are not large-group meetings. They are small-group meetings called by management. Managers summon their underlings for the purpose of consultation. They wish to stimulate a co-operative and productive workplace environment and to build team spirit. At the start of the meeting the manager briefly expounds his own point of view. When that hour is over the underlings expound their points of view. When that five minutes is over, so is the meeting.

Some people like meetings. They see themselves as ideas people. They go from meeting to meeting sowing ideas in the manner of a mayfly depositing eggs. Others do not see them as ideas people. They see them as people who don't do any work.

The most popular topic for discussion at any meeting is the topic that was discussed and not resolved at the last meeting. It is not resolved at this meeting either. Cue for the second most popular topic of discussion at meetings: the date of the next meeting. This discussion can occupy a remarkably large part of a meeting.

Managers often call meetings to ensure that things are being done. Calling the meeting ensures that, for the duration of the meeting, things stop being done. The people who are attending the meeting know that the things will still have to be done and that the meeting will not affect the way that they are done. It will affect only the amount of time available for getting them done.

In short meetings are rarely good things. They stop work being done, they arrive at predetermined decisions, they create the worst possible atmosphere for the generation of ideas, they cause resentment among the industrious, they are hijacked by fools and they gratify only the vacuous.

So when I ring a friend at work and am told that I cannot speak to him because he is in a meeting, I hope, for the sake of my friend, that I am being lied to. I hope that the only meeting he is attending is with porcelain or coffee. And I suspect I am often right.

I wish they didn't

It's a pity the Americans speak English. It makes it hard to see them as foreign. But foreign they are, as foreign as Turks, as Uzbeks.

It's absurd of course to discuss a quarter of a billion people as if they shared a common character, but at least I won't be hamstrung by facts. I know little.

Two weeks ago in Florida I rented a canoe. The canoe-renter was the authentic Southern thing – pick-up truck, moustache, cat hat and a drawl like dripping treacle. He told me he had always wanted to go to New Zealand. I said he should. He paused by the river to think in the intense gelatinous heat.

'Now would I have to be getting me a passport?'

I said he would.

'That's not a problem,' he said. 'And would I have to be changing my US dollars?'

I said he would.

'That's not a problem.'

He put the canoe into the water and me into the canoe. 'Now you all be having a nice paddle, do you hear me?'

I said I did and I would. And I did. Small alligators, big otters, pileated woodpeckers, snapping turtles, basking turtles, catfish and a spring-fed river as clear as Hemingway's prose. But most of the way down this river out of Eden I was preoccupied with thoughts of the canoe renter. What was it that made him American – for he could not have been anything else? Was it the courtesy, the affability, the insularity?

Years ago I travelled down the West Coast of the States – as far away from this Florida river as Brazil – and I travelled light. I carried only a backpack of prejudices. Cherished prejudices, racial heirlooms that I was unwilling to let go.

I had been raised to see Americans as energetic children, committed to making money and being keen, but all of them, in the words of Evelyn Waugh, who was and who remains my favourite bigot, 'exiles uprooted and doomed to sterility'.

After three weeks of thumbing and catching buses, I knew that either I had been sucked in or Waugh was wrong. These people were different, but if I had to choose a single adjective to describe them I would not choose sterile. I would choose good. These people were good.

The young did not seem disaffected. The old seemed free from bile. Their interest in me was all that I could wish and their generosity was greater than I could handle.

At the small town where I stayed last month in Florida the highest paid member of the university staff is the football coach. Each Saturday in winter 85,000 locals turn out to watch his team. It's a team of kids, 20 years old, too young to drink. Some of them weigh 300 pounds – in metric terms that translates to just over two people.

At game's end, win or lose, they kneel to pray. God's big in the

States, almost as big as the breakfasts. I love the pancakes. 'Short stack or tall stack?' they ask. A short stack is a meal for two. A tall stack is a meal for America. They beat the world in fat. They beat the world in bigness. They beat the world.

Paul's Diner was cheap and dark and empty, the pancakes syrup-drenched, the coffee thin but unlimited, the service uniquely courteous. It is an endlessly polite country. By the griddle a little placard. 'Praise the Lord,' it said.

I caught a bus to a shopping mall. The passengers were poor and black. They talked. They did not know each other but they talked. This was no English or New Zealand or French bus. This was more like a bus in India.

A girl nattered to the driver about her wedding. In the gaps in conversation she read at random from a book. The book was called *Prayers that Much Avail*.

I wanted books for the long flight home. In the whole monstrous air-conditioned shopping mall the only books I found were a ceiling-high stack of Bibles, King James version, both Old and New Testaments, nicely printed and a dollar each.

Hanging outside countless houses the stars and stripes. And written in windows and on placards jammed into lawns, the words 'God Bless America'. If anything sums the country up it's that strange slogan – part prayer, part statement. Somehow it lies at the heart of the huge and insular country that leads the world, a country that can relish Disney World, a bewildering engaging dazzle of a country, a country that seems bereft of irony until you watch the brilliance of *The Simpsons*, a country that made all the global running in the century just ended, a country that I know I do not know, a country that I wish did not speak English.

Be luggage

I like to think that I'm as sympathetic as the next chap, but there are limits. And beyond those limits stand rap musicians. Being middle-aged, middle-class and crusty as a pie, I find rap music unspeakable. But this week I have found myself in the unaccustomed position of feeling sorry for a rapster, oozing sympathy, indeed, like a wounded social worker. It can't go on.

I should stress at this point that the rapster I am feeling sorry for is not Mr Eminem. Apparently Mr Eminem is being sued. Some composer has claimed that he wrote the tune for 'Kill You', a sweet little ballad about murdering women, and that Mr Eminem stole it. But I don't think Mr Eminem has much to fear. He has only to play his music in court to be acquitted, not only of stealing a tune, but also of using one.

No, the rap chap I sympathise with is the one who went nuts on the plane. From what I can gather he tipped back 35 dutyfree rums, howled, leapt from his seat, upended a stewardess and sexually interfered with a drinks trolley before being overpowered by an excited purser and a posse of socially responsible passengers. Naturally I sympathise with the passengers' desire to rough the lout up, but the odd thing is that I also sympathise with the lout himself. He did precisely what I want to do on aeroplanes.

Forty-five years have taught me that the only proper way to travel is on foot, with one pair of underpants, an insouciant swagger and a knobkerrie for bopping the natives when they get frisky. It's arduous, painful and testing. If you don't fancy any of that you should stay at home and watch *Our World*. But sadly two bicycle repair men from North Carolina put paid to all that.

Orville and Wilbur Wright yearned to fly, if only to part company with the cruel world that had given them their Christian names. And in trying to build a plane they were following an ancient tradition. People have always fantasised about flight. Gods flew, mythical heroes flew, Icarus flew, Superman flew. But man didn't. Then the Wrights did. With their balsa wood and rice paper they made the dream flesh. That's always a mistake.

Sages down the centuries have been careful to stress that dreams are dreams and quite beyond our grasp. They have portrayed life on earth as a business of disappointment and baked beans, with the joy and caviar arriving only post mortem. Now, I have no way of knowing whether the sages are right about the post-mortem bit, but I do know that when people realise their dreams ante mortem, those dreams have a habit of turning to ashes in the mouth. And so it has proved with air travel. It is less than a century since the Wright brothers tinkered, but how the dream's turned bitter.

The horrors begin at the airport. Airports have no geographical location. They stand like pariah dogs beyond the city walls in wasteland that is neither rural nor urban. Bristle carpet, plate glass, a duty-free shop selling kiwifruit cremes, and gin in London-bus-shaped porcelain bottles, an accessory shop full of inflatable neck pillows and matching his and hers tartan overnight bags with little leads so they can be towed like rectilinear dogs, and an indigenous crafts shop selling, oh dear me, indigenous crafts. All of this stuff owes its existence only to airports and air travel. Take it out of your bag when you arrive and you wonder what suspended your judgment.

Airports even discourage walking. Little travelators carry you along the corridors of self-replicating synthetic materials, air-conditioning and muzak. The whole place is designed to work on you like anaesthesia. Because to an airline you are troublesome. They prefer your luggage. It weighs much the same as you do but it doesn't need feeding or heating or to be shown movies.

On board the technological bird you are pampered by people in toy-town uniforms. You are about to travel several thousand miles and they give you a pair of slippers. They feed you, tuck you up, answer your every whim, smile at you, require nothing of you but your passivity. It ought to be lovely but it isn't. Ancestral voices whisper in your ear that something's wrong. You are sitting down but moving. You are crossing oceans but are warm and dry. You are traversing continents but the view from the seat remains unchanged. You have lost control of your destiny. You have been reduced to luggage.

None of us likes to be luggage. In the end we are all of us, even rap musicians, autonomous beings . Hence the rapster's outburst and my unwonted sympathy for him. Though I suppose, on reflection, it is just possible that he was merely loud-mouthed, ill-mannered, boorish, spoilt, conceited, wrong and drunk.

Seven minutes to live

If you had seven minutes to live, how would you fill them? Would you make peace with your maker, perhaps, or just make a cup of tea and look at the sky, or even make love – though that would leave the problem of the other six minutes? Me, I'd make mayonnaise.

Delia Smith, the celebrated cook, makes mayonnaise in seven minutes flat. She's timed herself, she says, with a stopwatch. Well, everyone finds their own way of wringing pleasure from the world.

The supermarket shelves abound in ersatz mayonnaise, relying for their sales on Hollywood endorsements or an advertising budget equal to the GDP of Poland. But supermarket mayonnaise resembles the authentic stuff as I resemble Paul Newman.

Authentic mayonnaise has the consistency of shaving cream. It blobs, and each blob rises to a tip that slumps. The taste, however, is harder to define, indeed all taste is tough to do in words as the wine wallahs found out long ago. They tell us that a chardonnay has hints of passionfruit, but ask them to describe the taste of passionfruit and they'll be mute. The only certain thing is that it doesn't taste like wine.

The other week I was told by a frank and knowledgeable master of plonk that the tongue in not a very discriminating instrument. It can distinguish only between sweet and sour, and salt and whatever is the opposite of salt (which apparently isn't pepper). He said that all other tasting is done by the sense of smell, which is why when you are ravaged by a cold all food tastes of phlegm.

The taste of mayonnaise is especially elusive. It's as subtle as good flattery. At its best it tastes exquisitely of nothing. It's self-effacing, drawing attention to the brasher foods it complements. The nearest I can come to it are words from Katherine Mansfield on a similar foodstuff. 'Jose and Laura were licking their fingers,' wrote Mansfield in *The Garden Party*, 'with that absorbed inward look that only comes from whipped cream.'

This week I bought some flakes of that crabstick stuff that's fashioned from reconstituted bits of fish then decorated with a reddish tinge and given an authentic-sounding Japanese name, and when I brought it home and laid it on the kitchen bench I thought I heard a noise. I bent down close and caught the crabstick crying out for mayonnaise.

I knew that mayonnaise had eggs in it but that was all I knew. I hauled Delia from the shelves. It was nice to find a recipe requiring things I didn't have to go and buy. Eggs I had in abundance, plus oil and salt and pepper. Delia also called for mustard powder but that was clearly dispensable because (a) no mayonnaise I've met has tasted of mustard, (b) the quantity required was minute and (c) I didn't have any.

Delia told me first to separate an egg. I'd seen chefs do that on television. Television eggs, of course, are different – chefs crack them one-handed and never have to fish for errant bits of shell – but I took my egg and cracked it and slid the yolk from half shell to half shell until the white fell away to a brace of dogs who stood below with jaws agape like giant furry nestlings. My isolated yolk was the colour of that middle traffic light whose purpose I have never understood.

Then, said Delia, holding the electric beater in one hand and the bottle of oil in the other, add a single drop of oil and beat it in. I did as I was bid, holding the bowl still with the third hand that Delia had forgotten. Then another drop of oil, and another and another, beating all the while like an old-fashioned schoolmaster. To my surprise, and just as Delia said it would, the mixture suddenly thickened and resembled mayonnaise. And at that point, said Delia, I'd passed the time of danger and could add a slug of oil. I added a slug of oil. The mixture turned to sludge.

Not to worry, said Delia. Feed the dogs another egg white, and add the sludge to the new yolk drop by drop until it thickens again. I did as bid and watched it thicken, then added a slug of oil.

For the next egg I had to go out to the henhouse, but by now I had learnt caution. Slugs were out and dribbles in. In time I had a bowl of three-egg mayonnaise as rich as Mr Getty, and the crabstick sandwich that it featured in was, as they say, to die for. And had I had seven minutes to live I would have died for it about an hour before I ate it.

He was a pretty good dog

Around midnight last night I went up the hill with my dogs, one of them walking beside me unusually subdued, the other one in a bag over my shoulder, dead. I carried a spade. I knew the spot where I wanted to bury him. Nothing special about it, but some distance from the path so that the grave would not be disturbed.

The hill is steep. The dogs and I have climbed it perhaps a thousand times. I usually stop at a couple of places to pant, and three-legged Abel would always stop beside me, panting too.

He was a big dog, 30 kilos or so, more than half a hundred-weight. The straps of the bag bit into my right shoulder and I walked in a slewed hunch, climbing perhaps 20 yards at a time and then pausing for breath. But I didn't unsling him from my shoulder. It would have seemed disloyal.

When I came home at 9 o'clock last night he was waiting for me. He whined with pleasure as I got out of the car. I could hear his tail thumping the deck. But when I opened the gate he didn't come to me. I went to him and he was on his haunches. He tried to get up but his one back leg buckled and he sat down again. I put my hand to the leg and he nuzzled at the hand to keep it away from the point of pain.

I went inside. As I knew he would, he dragged himself to the space under my desk that was his den. For obvious ancestral reasons dogs take comfort from a den. My other dog joined him and I lay on the floor and stroked the pair of them together and whispered to them. Then I rang the vet.

On the phone the vet said he thought it would be a problem with a disc that he could fix with cortisone. I doubted it but I didn't say so. I lay with the dogs until the vet arrived.

When Abel heard the car he sat up and barked. The vet examined the leg and tapped the knee with a little rubber hammer and then drove back to his surgery to fetch the drugs that kill. While we waited Abel licked my face a lot.

I rang a friend who looks after the dogs when I'm away and told her what was happening. She arrived before the vet returned and from the floor Abel greeted her with glee.

The vet sedated him with an injection in the scruff of the neck. A quarter of an hour later when the dog's head had sunk onto his paws and his eyelids drooped, the vet tied a tourniquet around the knee of the right front leg, shaved a little fur from the shin, found a vein and inserted the needle. The dog looked at the needle with drowsy curiosity. I said I would like to take over from there.

There was a little blood in the barrel of the syringe, swirling slowly in the bright blue barbiturates. I pressed the plunger and my dog slumped immediately onto his side. I stroked his ears and the top of his head and his flanks and the band of darker fur that ran from his muzzle and up between his eyes. I asked if he was dead and the vet checked the eyes and gums. The pupils had dilated and the gums turned purple.

It took half an hour or so to lug him up the hill. January 31st was a warm night, with a butter-yellow almost full moon, and by the time I started digging, my shirt was soaked with sweat. At the place I had chosen to bury him the topsoil was only 6 inches deep. My spade rang against rock. I tried a few yards to either side but it was the same.

I picked him up again, still in the bag with his head lolling life-like from the opening, and I went over the ridge and dug again. At the third attempt I found deep enough soil and I dug for a long time down into the clay.

His tongue was sticking out so I opened his jaws and eased the tongue back. Then I lifted him from the bag and kissed him and laid him as gently as I could in the hole, folding his legs so that he looked all right. His eyes were open. I closed them and they opened again. I sprinkled earth over his body and then over his face, and then because I didn't like to use the spade I scooped the rest of the earth in with my hands. I trod the grave down softly, then sat and looked out over the harbour and the dark hills and smoked a cig-arette. The sweat cooling on my shirt made me shiver. Then I went down the hill with one dog.

Lotsadeadredindians

Nicols Fox has written a book called *Against the Machine* in which she puts the case against labour-saving domestic gadgets.

Some years ago her clothes-drier broke down and she was forced to peg clothes on a line. 'I discovered that the trip outside to the clothesline forced me to interact with the day in a new way . . . Now I hang clothes outside every day, even in the Maine winter.'

Ms Fox is especially harsh on dishwashers. She recalls her idyllic childhood in backwoods America – I forget the actual name of the place but Lotsadeadredindians will do – where 'my mother and grandmother and I used to wash the dishes together in the kitchen and we had a lot of really good conversations in the process. They passed along stories and lessons for life . . . washing dishes wasn't just washing dishes. It was a kind of event.'

For Ms Fox, the dishwasher not only discourages such inter-generational exchange but also 'robs you of the only interesting aspect of dishwashing which is how to get off that piece of cheese that's stuck to the plate'.

A bestseller in paperback, *Against the Machine* has now been made into a play. And in a scoop I present the first scene.

Location – a kitchen in a log cabin in Lotsadeadredindians.

Cast – Nicols Fox as a girl and Grandma Bristlechin.

Action – the dishes.

Grandma Bristlechin: Why look you here, my child.

Nicols: What is it, Grandmama

Grandma Bristlechin: Just you look at that. Oh me oh my, if that ain't the most interesting piece of cheese I've seen stuck to a plate in many a long year I'll eat the rim off my stetson and boil the rest of it into an apple-pie for Thanksgiving.

Nicols: Grandmama, can I ask you a question in the interests of pursuing an intergenerational conversation?

Grsndma Bristlechin: You go right ahead, my child, while I gets a-scraping with this here knuckle bone that's somehow become exposed through 103 years of washing dishes.

Nicols: What's menstruation?

Pause.

Nicols: Grandmama?

Grandma Bristlechin: What is it, my li'l potato dumpling?

Nicols: I asked you an intergenerational question in order to give you the opportunity to pass on a story or a lesson for life and you didn't say nothing, Grandmama.

Grandma Bristlechin: Well, bless me, my child. I guess I just got too carried away with this here interesting morsel of cheese.

Nicols: Grandmama, why was I given such a ridiculous Christian name?

Grandma Bristlechin: My, you're full of questions for a li'l girl. Any fuller and your freckles'll pop off and vour dungarees bust and that's not something should happen afore the apples are safely in the barn and . . .

Nicols: Is this a story or a lesson lor life, Grandmama?

Grandma Bristlechin: There you go again, child. Why not go ask your momma. She's outside at the clothesline interacting with the day.

Nicols: But Grandmama, there's three foot of snow on the ground.

Grandma Bristlechin: Once a woman discovers pegging out there ain't no snowdrift in the whole of Lotsadeadredindians gonna put her off her daily interaction. But maybe by rights you should be fetching her in now afore she comes over all brittle again. *(Exit Nicols.)* Whoa, steady there, my child. What with all that energy of yourn you'll be a-tripping over the chain that's bound me to this sink for 103 years, the chain I do love so much I bless every li'l festering ulcer on my pretty ankle.

(Re-enter Nicols dragging her stiff blue mother whom she props against the dado.)

Nicols: Grandmama, what's a dado?

Grandma Bristlechin: There you go again, asking them questions of yourn. I swear there's more questions in you than there's crackers in that there weevil barrel.

Nicols: It's just the stage directions told me to prop Mother against it.

Grandma Bristlechin: Oh my child, move her this minute or she'll be a-dripping again and drenching the wainscoting.

Nicols (thoughtfully as she moves Mother to the larder): Grandmama, when I grow up I'm going to write a book and I'll become famous and rich and then I'll buy you a dishwasher and . . .

Grandma Bristlechin (snatching up her granddaughter and rubbing her fiercely across her chin until she draws blood): Now there'll be no more of that devil's talk from you, my child, or I'll be washing your mouth out with pork fat and sourdough, do you hear me? Where did you go learning them dirty words like dishwasher from? Why the dishwasher ain't even been invented yet and to tell the truth I ain't rightly sure it should be. Anyway I won't be having none under my roof, nor any of that clothes-drier business I heard you whispering about with young Jack Thimbleshift under the haybarn the other day. I'm onto you my girl, don't you worry.

Nicols wriggles out of Grandma Bristlechin's grasp and runs off stage right defiantly screaming, 'Clothes-drier, dishwasher, other labour-saving devices' while Grandma Bristlechin reaches calmly under the sink for her Smith & Wesson .303 and takes careful aim offstage. Curtain. Under the curtain a puddle forms as Momma thaws in time for Scene 2 in which Nicols begins to revise her position on gadgetry.

Big cherub

Sometimes I think of Michael Catt.

I wonder how he is and what he's up to. Whether he's selling real estate or training to be a plumber. Or whether, and this seems to be more likely, he's retired to a cottage in the mountains in some obscure and unvisited country, Lithuania, say, to read books of an escapist nature behind walls topped with razor wire.

Because Michael Catt was the English rugby player who half a dozen years ago was erased by Jonah Lomu. Even if you live in Lapland and smoke fish, even if you're a director of feminist studies, or even if your mind is wandering in a rest home that smells of disinfectant, you will have seen the tape.

The giant Lomu, puffing his cheeks like one of those cherubs in the corners of old maps, bore down on the English try line. He shrugged off tacklers as if they were so many cobwebs. One stood square in his way but succeeded in impeding the giant's momentum to about the same extent as a garden wall impedes a bulldozer. Lomu simply lowered his shoulder, braced his body and then proceeded over the rubble.

And finally in front of him stood Michael Catt, alone on a thin white line. Michael Catt adopted the position, the position they had taught him at school, the crouching position from which you launch a tackle on an oncoming opponent, driving with your legs and placing your head to the side of the body and . . . Lomu simply went both through and over Michael Catt. He chose to inhabit the space that Michael Catt had thought was his, and with the commentator memorably forsaking speech in favour of a series of gasps that shortened and quickened and overtook each other as if he, the commentator, were approaching sexual climax, Lomu scored the try. And in doing so he wrote Michael Catt into the catalogue of memorable images, images that are the common property of the world: Armstrong on the moon, the slumping Kennedy, the man and the tank in Tiananmen Square.

Life today cannot be easy for Michael Catt. In the Lithuanian corner shop the women in headscarves will pause in their perusal of the rollmop herrings and nudge and point and ask each other whether that isn't the poor chap who . . . For Michael Catt exists in the public mind as the frontispiece in Jonah's book of fame. Though an international rugby player in his own right he is known to millions only as the man who fell that another should rise.

Jonah's fans are not primarily rugby players. They are children who like Superman. And at heart we are all children who like Superman. In a decade of rugby Lomu has given us half a dozen glimpses of the human body taken to a new dimension. He's as near as reality has come to the Ubermensch, six-gun Arnie, the Hydra-slaying Hercules, the muscled superhero of the comic strips and a thousand identical video games. Hence the clamouring excited mobs, the mobs in London, the mobs in Paris, the mobs everywhere he goes. He is a myth made flesh. His pneumatic thighs are objects of reverence.

A poor child, from an immigrant underclass, he found success through physique. And now men from the overclass, men in ties, come flocking to hear him speak and to laugh with propitiatory willingness at his jokes. But in truth the men don't come to hear him. They come only to be near him, to be in his presence.

I've never met the man but he seems to be good. So far he has stayed loyal to New Zealand, resisting blandishments no doubt from every country in the world where rugby is played and where there is money. He is rich but he could have been many times richer.

And yet he retains something of his mean-streets heritage. He drives the sort of car I can neither understand nor condone, a low-slung throatmobile, with a boombox in the back that can shatter paving slabs. And he wears a tuft on his shaven head that on anyone else would look silly. On a superhero it looks apt.

There is also something endearing about him. I saw him interviewed some years ago about his clandestine wedding. The interviewer asked him questions in the tone one would use to a child lost in a shopping mall. It was nauseating, intrusive, wrong – and faultless tabloid television. The big man wept. The ad break was delayed as the camera zoomed in on the ratings.

I have heard Lomu called a genius. He is not a genius. Despite ten years of coaching by the best in the land he still passes, catches, kicks and tackles with little more skill than the average club player and he seems to have learnt no new tricks. But when he runs at people, the crowd rise to their feet as one and roar without knowing that they're roaring. They're roaring at a myth on the move. They're roaring for the man in front of him to crumple. They're roaring for another flattened Catt.

Land you can play with

Cold rain drilled the roof all day. I didn't notice when it stopped. Now, mid-evening, my duties done, I am horizontal on the sofa, head propped on a dirty cushion, a fat book on my chest. My dog has wrapped herself twice about the gas fire, singeing her belly-fur. The deep luxurious cocoon of winter.

There seems too much light at the window. I roll off the sofa, push back the blind. Snow. Dropping past the window in big, slow flakes. My heart lifts like a child's heart.

I have never believed that the Eskimos have eighty-seven words for snow. You need only one word. Snow. Listen to it. It sounds like snow.

Snow settles here perhaps twice a decade. It's the guest that visits rarely, surprisingly, and everywhere, in slippers. It takes a known landscape and makes it new.

And you have to be the first to defile it. I can no more resist snow than I can resist the best people. Boots, hat. My dog rises and stretches. She doesn't know what's beyond the door. She has seen snow only once before. A puppy then, she danced and snorted in it, unable to grasp the nature of a world new-made. I open the door and we stand at the threshold of the white world like two children. Like Adam and Eve.

She hesitates, sniffs the snow, advances into it and then we're off up the untouched road. As we climb I turn to look at the black wet marks of my boots and her paws and I think Robinson Crusoe. Then on to the hills.

Snow is land that you can play with. I toss a snowball. It hits a bush and disintegrates. My dog rushes to fetch it and cannot find it. I toss another. She jumps to catch it in the air, bites it and I hear her jaws clash. She sneezes and shakes her head and her body writhes with the game. I toss more and more. She leaps for each one, and bites through it.

The snow falls on my sweater and melts into black. It falls on her fur and stays white until she shakes it off. It is falling in big wet flakes. Further up the hill it forms miniature drifts in the grass. It bends the stems of ragwort, the brushes of broom. Though my hands are numb I cannot resist its texture. I throw snowballs at fenceposts. I strike the branches of trees and then scamper backwards out of the mini-blizzard, shaking myself like a dog.

On the hills deep silence, a giant muffling. I think that I can hear the snowflakes landing. And underfoot the stuff squeaks. Through the cloud the moon shows phosphorescent-oily. The snow won't let the light sink into the land. It tosses it back and gleams. The hills are sharp-edged.

I stop to look down over the white roofs of Lyttelton. I can hear children emerging to squeal and slide and fall and cry. The snow is a better and more unexpected gift than Christmas.

Over a fence and a ridge and then down the side of a silent valley to visit my old dog's grave. I've piled rocks there. I don't disturb their cap of snow. I stand a while. The wet has seeped through my boots, soaked my socks, is starting to numb my toes. I don't much mind. The feeling is as memory-laden as a smell.

The snow has stopped. I urge it to start again. Going back down the hill my boot whips out from under me and I am suddenly heavily on my back. Jarred. Up-ended like a circus clown. Snow's anarchic, a worldwide banana skin. It sends trucks slewing, sends wheels spinning suddenly useless. With heavy slow insistence it breaks our cables, saps our power, defeats us, makes us fools.

I am not hurt. Snow tossed me over but broke my fall. I lie a while. My dog waits with animal patience. At the foot of the path a house. Guests are leaving. The open front door glows golden like a Christmas card. Voices are excited by the snow. 'Be careful now. Be careful.' The snow magnifies the sound, reflects it as it reflects light. I put my dog on the lead. There's a puppyish zest in her.

While we've been up the hill a mass of people have trodden the road, all doing as we've done. The snow is soiled and ruined slush. Past a house where a neighbour sits with his son. They have double glazing, never draw their curtains. They are watching television.

Rain starts to fall, pitting the snow. In the morning it will have gone.

Dreams on wheels

My mother drives a hatchback. It's the sort of car in which you have to press the throttle to find out if the engine's running.

Two months ago my mother was taking me for a drive when a sports car overtook us. It was a sixties MG, all bucket seats and adolescence revisited. Like all sports cars it was designed to appeal to men too old to play sport.

As the MG passed, my mother sighed. 'Oh,' she said, 'I'd just love one of those.' My mother is seventy-nine. Naturally I was appalled.

I had thought my mother immune to whim. She belongs to a generation that did not indulge itself. Women like her wore printed cotton frocks and devoted their lives to rearing large families on carbohydrates and a single income.

To learn that even my mother could lust in secret for a car, underlined a truth of affluent society. Every vehicle is a wheeled aspiration. Every vehicle reflects its owner.

Most young men want a motor bike. A motor bike equates to freedom. It is the horsepower that snaps the apron strings, the oyster-knife that shucks open the world. It is wind in the hair and a throb between the legs. Whether or not a young man gets a motor bike depends on how much his parents dislike him.

My own motor bike was a moped. It went up hill quite well if you pedalled it. I loved that bike. I used to sing on it. I sang songs rich with adolescent grief or adolescent rapture. I bellowed my new-found manhood to the overarching sky. Once I swallowed a wasp. It made me crash. I had no excuse for my other crashes.

There are three ways to stop riding motor bikcs. One is to do yourself damage. Another is to grow up. The third is to yield your motor bike to the police. I took the third option. As a result I missed the next phase of motorised life – the young person's car.

Young people drive heaps or phalluses. The heap is cheap, is poverty on wheels. It has rust, and vinyl, and keyless entry through the rear passenger window. You can sleep in a heap, or have sex in it, or tell lies about having sex in it. The heap is yesterday's car for tomorrow's people.

The phallus is tomorrow's car for today's hooligans. It's an enclosed motor bike. Based on designs for Apollo XVI its bonnet is longer than its passenger cell. It has fat tyres, gulping air intakes, a boombox, a fiercely farting exhaust and a spoiler at the back. The spoiler is named after the parents who paid for the car.

But the bike, the heap and the phallus are just rungs on the ladder towards middle age. Middle age is compromise and so is its car. That car is a saloon. It's the motorised equivalent of clothes from Farmer's. Though manufacturers take pains to promote the differences between saloons, the whole point of them is their sim-ilarity. Practical, sensible and dull as a suburb, saloons refuse to poke their heads above the parapet of conformity.

But there are alternatives. Those who have encumbered themselves with a vast brood forsake even the aerodynamic hints of a saloon. They acquire a people-carrier. It's a nine-seater semi-bus. It battles through the wind towards the future. The people-carrier announces to the world that the owner has surrendered all claim to independent personal life.

More assertive is the four-wheel drive all-terrain recreational vehicle. Rectilinear and butch, it resembles a shipping container on stilts. The owner still wants to compete. On the front a monstrous pair of bullbars to scatter rampaging herds of supermarket trolleys.

Beyond the all-terrain butchness comes the executive smoothness. Smug as a bank account, sleek as a suit, it glides from home to office, climate-controlled, equipped with everything, a motorised Switzerland, self-contained, neutral, unassailable, purring with pleasure at itself.

But all is vanity and in the end the king of the road is time. Time makes people old and as they grow old they shrink. Their cars shrink with them. They shrink to those strange elevated narrow cars. They shrink to hatchbacks.

So when my mother said she yearned for a sports car, I gawped. I had never dreamed that she dreamed. But magnanimity is everything. 'Mother dear,' I said, 'old age should do as old age wishes. Mortgage the house, squander my inheritance, scour the country for a pink MG and scandalise the neighbours. Set the net curtains twitching and the tongues aclack. You are only old once. Follow your dreams. Buy that car.'

My mother looked at me. 'But I couldn't get in or out of it,' she said. So all, in the end, was well.

All squared away

It's all over. The final whistle's blown. I've lost, they've won and that's that. I've bought an iron.

Who 'they' are is hard to define. Call them the forces of conformity if you like but I think there's more to them than that. The forces come from within as much as without. My mind's been fingering the notion of an iron for several months. And just as when a customer fingers an item in a store, drifts elsewhere, then sidles back to finger it once more, and the alert shopkeeper knows that the thing is effectively sold, well, so it has proved with my iron. I am forty-five years old. My laundry cycle is finally complete.

Once upon a time in the lala land of infancy I had the knack of laundry. I gave it to my mother. She took it rumpled and soiled and gave it back smooth and smelling of air. But when I left home I forgot to take her with me. I also forgot to thank her. For I don't know how many handkerchiefs ironed square. For limitless pairs of cricket trousers with creases down the front, the grass stains on the knee scrubbed with a nail brush to faint brown ghosts of themselves.

For the next decade or so laundry bedevilled me. I delayed the doing of it. I would rescue T-shirts from the floor, sniff at their armpits and if my nose didn't wrinkle like a boxer dog's I'd steal another day. But eventually every T-shirt would be soiled to unwearability, every underpant to unspeakability and into a great black bin liner went the lot, into my pocket went a stash of change, and I would trudge all hunched and burdened to the laundrette.

Laundrettes the world over were identical. Crouched in some shaded part of town they never bothered to promote themselves with neon signs or advertising because the owner knew that if you didn't need to come you never would, but if you did, however horrible it was, you had no choice.

The streets they occupied were thick with litter and feral children and bitter urban misery. The single room was asthmatic with steam, as if the Amazon had been top-dressed with detergent. The machines were built industrially strong to stand the attentions of the poor of spirit. Above them notices explained in the simplest terms the modes of operation. You never read the notices. All machines worked the same. They had a little push-in tray with slots for coins. You emptied out your bin liner, holding your breath against the sudden pot-pourri of stale human emanations, then went outside to smoke and walk the desperate suburbs of the city for half an hour.

There were always enough washers. There were never enough driers. With your wet pile you stationed yourself in front of the drier with the least time to run on its dial. If the laundrette was empty the urge to cheat was fierce, to haul the unknown other's washing from the drier half done. The truly bold and cunning stopped two driers at once, emptied the first, transferred the washing from the second to the first, then placed his own in the second. I never dared.

I simply waited. It was longer than hospital waiting. When finally the drier fell to silence and either the proprietor claimed his washing or I, with slight distaste, unloaded the clothes, edgy with static, dumped them all unfolded in a pile – acceptable within the etiquette of laundrettes – and replaced them with my own I knew with slight relief that I was nearing bliss. The bliss of clean clothes. The bliss of a fortnight of freedom, a fortnight that would trickle by and as it trickled so the weight of dread would build, the knowledge that I'd soon once more have to revisit the stews of despair.

But then at thirty I tossed out my bin liner, stopped collecting change and bought a house. It came with a second-hand washing machine. I've got it still. I bless it.

But I never got an iron. If sometimes people pointed out the crumples in my shirts I said I didn't iron because my body wasn't square. I lied. I didn't iron because I didn't know how. And I didn't learn how because I was lazy. But, most significantly of all, I didn't iron because I didn't feel the need.

Why then should I now have fallen? Why in middle age should I spend time beside my jauntily striped Briscoes ironing board, squirting jets of steam on shirts and flattening the cloth? Is it just the gradual erosion into middle-class conformity? Perhaps it is. I never was a rebel. But I think there's something more to it than that. I think it may just be that I have bought an iron because I've noticed that my skin's begun to crease.

At two drunks swimming

As any safety enthusiast will tell you, drinking and swimming don't mix. And as any drunk will tell the safety enthusiast, nuts.

The safety wallah will say that out of every thousand drunks who go swimming, one drowns. The drunk will say that he's never seen a thousand drunks swimming.

Anyway, there were only two of us, so it was a statistical near-certainty that the drunk who drowns was still in the pub. Well, actually, there were four of us, if you include the dogs, and we did.

The trip to the bay was the barman's idea. My other excuses are that I was drunk, that my dog likes swimming, that I like swimming with her, that it had been a hot day, and that it was midnight.

The problem with a hot day is that it doesn't happen at midnight. A southerly had risen. The waves were a couple of feet tall and fringed with cream. But we were committed, and the dogs were exultant.

The barman stood on the rail of the jetty in his trendy swimming togs. I stood on the bottom step of the jetty in my sky-blue Warehouse underpants. The barman finished his cigarette, tossed it into the sea in a glowing arc and followed it. I finished my cigarette, tossed it into the sea in a glowing arc and stayed where I was.

The coolest man I ever saw was standing on the high board above a French swimming pool, smoking. He had the body of a decathlete. People were looking up at him. He knew they were looking up at him. When he neared the end of his cigarette he wrapped his tongue round the filter, withdrew it into his mouth and dived. Then he surfaced, rolled onto his back, unfurled his tongue and carried on smoking.

From the water the barman called his dog. The dog is young, loyal and stupid. While I stood admiring the goosebumps on my arms, it bounded past me and launched itself. Dogs dive badly. They start paddling before they hit the water. And they land on their bellies.

The smack when the dog hit the water made me wince. The dog did not wince. It was away, black and happy in the black water.

I was not away. I called to the swimming barman to count down from three. On three, I crouched. On two, I breathed in. On one, I swung my arms back. On go, I stood up again. The barman said something provocative. I dived. The water was surprisingly warm. My sky-blue Warehouse underpants came off.

My dog appeared beside me, her legs frantic under the water. She snorts as she swims, but she can swim for miles. I can't.

All females float. Nine out of ten white males float. I am the tenth. If I lie still in water I sink. Apparently most black men sink too. I suppose that is why you see few black swimmers in the Olympics.

At the same time, you see lots of black runners. The conclusion to draw, I suppose, is that if you're a white man being chased by a black man, you should head for water. If you're a black man being chased by a white man, run. And if you've got one white parent and one black parent, you should be fine.

I didn't suppose all this at the time. I was trying to swim towards a raft anchored in the middle of the bay. It went in and out of view with the waves. I got mouthfuls of salt.

I lost my dog behind a wave and I worried about her. Then I felt a twinge of cramp in my calf and I worried about me. The raft seemed a long way away.

I hate seaweed. When it slithers against my chest it reminds me of the depths of black water below. I do not like to be so reminded. I can think of few deaths worse than drowning. People say that your life passes in front of your eyes. Perhaps it does, but with water in my airways I doubt if I'd sit back with popcorn to watch it. Anyway, I've seen it before.

People also say drowning is peaceful. I don't know how they know. And of all the opposites of peaceful, one of the most emphatic is having water in your airways.

I veered towards the shore. I couldn't see my dog, or the barman's dog, or the barman, or any pleasure in what I was doing. I wanted solidity under me. I was fighting the water and panic.

I heard barking and saw my dog on the path above me. That made the last ten yards easy. I hauled myself onto the rocks like something primeval evolving. My dog fussed about me. I picked my way along the gravel path towards my clothes, naked, teeth chattering like a typewriter, acutely aware of being Lear's 'poor bare forked animal'.

The barman had swum to the raft and back.

'Great, wasn't it,' he said.

I said I'd been scared.

'Yeah,' he said, 'great, isn't it.' And I had to admit that it was. Afterwards. Scared is good, afterwards.

Girlie sox

Are you a sturdy independent, one who stands strong and rooted when the winds of fashion blow, one who disdains the mob, who proclaims 'no coward soul is mine', who stands for what he stands for and who rises above fad? Me too. And yet I've bought three pairs of girlie socks.

Girlie socks are the socks you wear when you pretend not to be wearing socks. Professional female tennis players have always worn girlie socks. And although professional female tennis players grow more muscular every year, and although they grunt like mastodons – or at least how I imagine mastodons would have grunted, which is effortfully – they still, the tennis players that is and not the mastodons, wear girlie socks. At their girliest these socks have a pink bobble on the back to stop the sock shrivelling into the shoe.

My girlie socks do not have a pink bobble on the back. Nevertheless I cannot deny their girliness. Nor can I pretend they are an error. I drove to the Warehouse, strode through home appliances and stationery and reached menswear after a mere fifteen minutes. I studied the sock racks. I fingered and I pondered. For as long as I have been buying my own socks the result of this exercise has never varied. I have come away from the store with emphatically non-girlie socks. But not any more.

I can understand why female tennis players wear girlie socks. By being hidden in the shoe, girlie socks make legs look longer. Longer legs are sexier legs. What is harder to understand is why I should now wear them. My legs are as long as they need to be. Though they satisfactorily link my buttocks to my feet, my legs do not excite me and forty-five years of experience suggest that I would be unwise to expect them to excite others. Nevertheless I have now encased the southern ends of those legs in long-leg-making girlie socks.

Since I was seventeen I have played squash in the sort of white ankle socks that used car salesmen in the eighties wore with slip-on shoes. I am pleased to report that the car salesmen have forsaken those socks, but I have persisted with them for squash. I have found them cheap and satisfactory.

They are made in some factory in Pakistan or Taiwan where the workers earn a dollar a day. I have never cared about these workers because I have never met them. If I did meet them I imagine that I would still not care.

I have worn a thousand pairs of their socks until the heel in each has withered from a cushion of fluff to a transparent but indestructible lattice of nylon. When a sock reaches that point I put it in a drawer. Five years later I come across it curled and grey like corpse skin, and I throw it away. But each sock has done its duty. Honest traditional ankle socks, convenient, cheap, serving their purpose, the dull foot soldiers in the hosiery war. But now I have forsaken them for girlie socks.

Money does not explain my change of heart. Girlie and non-girlie socks were the same price. Colour does not come into it either. White is white. A man with whom I used to play squash, now cruelly killed by cancer, used to play in unmatching fluorescent socks. But though I admired him and though he regularly beat me and laughed as he did so, I could never emulate him. I am a white sock man.

The only reason I can offer for my shift into girlie socks is, well, take down your photo album. Turn, if you are old enough, to the seventies. Stare at the flares and the hair and the chunky shoes and the cheesecloth shirt with the tear-drop collar. Or the hotpants or the maxi-skirt or the, well, you get the picture. Indeed you've got the picture. For once the camera, source of a million lies, doesn't lie.

To put it with cruel simplicity, I bought my girlie socks because they are the fashion and other men have started wearing them. And though I have openly scoffed at those men, and though I have rightly observed that girlie socks offer no advantages over ankle socks, nevertheless, gradually, regrettably, but inevitably, I have come to see my ankle socks as staid, as ugly, as the sporting equivalent of the knee-length walk socks of the holidaying bureaucrat.

Have you ever seen a million starlings coming in to roost at dusk? They wheel like a living cloud, darkening the sky, forming one minute a spinning upward vortex, the next a diving arrowhead, driven by God knows what imperative and all of them squealing. Listen closely to that squeal. 'No coward soul is mine,' proclaims each starling. 'I am a sturdy independent.'

Oi Popey-boy

I can't be bothered with interviewing people any more. Most of the people worth interviewing are dead.

But interviews abound. Interviews with pustular rock stars, installation artists, skeletal fashion models, subliterate Hollywood marionettes, quivering novelists with bad breath, footballers.

And the trouble is, of course, that everyone's so flattered to be interviewed that they imagine they must have some thoughts worth attending to and so they spend a day thinking a few up. Then they deliver same with such sonorous earnestness – 'Frankly I see my art works as a search for identity, creating a fusion from the different ways of seeing inherent in our cultural diversity' – that it's all I can do to keep my breakfast down.

Besides it's such a hassle organising an interview, ringing up, say, the Pope and trying to persuade him to nip down to the Volcano for a chat. And then when he does agree there's even more hassle about how to hide security guards behind the Bill Hammonds, what to feed the sniffer dogs, and the exact design of chalice that the Pope's going to swill his Monteiths from, so in the end I always sighingly agree to fly to Rome and to be ushered into the Papal presence as if it were some sort of marquee, a marquee thronged with chubby cardinals and other corporate executives of Him Upstairs. And given the lack of Monteiths and the abundance of circumambient cardinals with ears like tuning-forks, the Pope is always on his best behaviour and simply trots out the party line as laid out in the mission statement sent to all stakeholders a couple of thousand years ago.

So I've resolved to change all that. Henceforth I shall conduct all interviews, as many as three a day, in bed and alone. It's quicker, easier and it gets straight to the truth. Here, for example, is the complete and unedited transcript of the first interview of a series of one, conducted in bed with the Pope shortly after the alarm went off this morning at the crack of ten. It was all over by five past. Efficiency, see.

Me: Oi Popey-boy.

Pope (kneeling, fumbling for a ring to kiss, before I cuff him playfully away): Oh, Your Journalosity. May I say how honoured I am? And with regard to your bid for canonisation . . .

Me: Bid! Let's get this one straight for starters, my preachy pal. When I fancy canonisation I won't be doing any bidding. I'll be instructing. Canonisation, I'll say, and the gun will go off and that will be that. Capisch?

Pope: I'd prefer a flat white.

Me: Coming right up. Meanwhile I've got a short message and I want you to listen up good. You with me?

Pope: Being with you is a privilege, Your Columnness.

Me: Right. Good. Now stop it.

Pope: Stop what?

Me: It. All of it. This religion stuff. It won't do and you know it.

It was okay once, laying down the moral law in a lawless time, trying to put an end to the tribal blood feuds and all that (though a glance at the Middle East doesn't suggest much in the way of success) but the point is it just won't wash any more.

Pope: Why are you picking on me?

Me: I'm not picking on you. I've got the rest of them lined up outside this bedroom door right this minute – archbishops, chief moderators, Archimandrites, televangelists, the lot. You just happened to be first because, well, I like you, Popey. I've said so in print before now and I don't retract a word of it, but nevertheless it's time to pull the plug.

Pope: But . . .

Me: But is not a word I'm fond of, Popey-boy. This isn't a discussion. This is an audience. So audiate away, my lad of the cloth, and audiate good. I want you to go forth and dismantle the whole shebang. Chasubles, rhythm methods, dog collars, waddling cardinals, the lot. Send it all down the same road as the sun-worship of the Aztecs. I'm not blaming you for all the empire building of the past, for the squillion heathen corpses slaughtered in the name of the boss, for siding with the rich against the poor and all the other ghastlies of yesterday, nor indeed for the retail monstrosity of Christmas, but I am saying that we need to ditch it all now. I mean it's no help when the head honcho of Bushbaby's own church comes out against the war on Iraq on the grounds of scriptural interpretation. Right answer but wrong method. Time to acknowledge, old son, and I know you won't take this the wrong way, the randomness of the world, the pointless atomic structure spinning in a void, and that if we're going to make a go of it we've got to accept there's no authority to fall back on and that it's up to us. All your lot do is cloud the issue. Think comic cosmic irony of purposelessness. Got it?

Pope: Yes.

Me: Good. Now dry your eyes and off you go. Just get out there and sack a few cardinals and you'll feel a whole lot better. Okay?

Pope: Thank you.

Me: A pleasure. Next! Ah, Ayatollah. Come in. Sit down. And listen up.

Shock revelations

In a shock revelation today the formula one world champion explained his success. 'I won because I've got the best car,' he said. 'It goes faster than the other cars and it doesn't break down. If I swapped cars with any of the other guys they'd win.'

When questioned about the shock revelation, a spokesman for the formula one governing body said he didn't know if the champion was telling the truth. 'And to be honest,' he added in a shock revelation, 'I don't care. Our concern is with making money. We do this through sponsorship and advertising and television rights. I have no idea why people want to watch motor racing myself, but as long as they do we're happy to advertise cigarettes and condoms to them.'

A spokesman for the formula one fan club said that he and his friends knew exactly why they liked watching motor racing. 'It's really primitive and stupid,' he said in a shock revelation. 'We like the speed and the noise and the association with glamour and the media hype. Plus there's always the chance of seeing someone killed. That's why we gather at the bends.'

'Death is popular,' confirmed the head of television news in a shock revelation. 'Every day we scour the wires for film of a disaster. The world's a big dangerous place, thank God. We normally find something. Our viewers love it. A good crash is excellent for ratings. That way we can charge more for advertising. Of course if there isn't film of it, it isn't news.'

In response to questioning he agreed that the highlight this week had been the airshow crash in, well, to be honest, he couldn't remember exactly where. 'But that doesn't matter at all,' he said in a shock revelation. 'Our viewers aren't there for information. It was great footage. We ran it four or five times in slow motion.'

'No, I can't remember where the airshow crash happened,' said a spokeswoman for the television news viewers association in a shock revelation, 'but I would like to stress that addicts of the six o'clock news are good conservative people. We think we deplore violence, so we do like to have it presented under the guise of information. It's also comforting to have news readers we like. Somehow we feel we can trust them. Infomercials work on the same principle, you know. That's why people fall for them.'

A fitness instructor confirmed the success of infomercials especially for exercise equipment. 'But,' he added in a shock revelation, rolling up his T-shirt and playing the 'Star-Spangled Banner' on his stomach with a pair of xylophone hammers, 'no one who buys our equipment ever gets abs like mine. In fact we don't expect our exercise equipment to be used for more than a day or two. It's designed to be folded away and forgotten. We have exciting plans,' he added, lowering his voice in an extra shock revelation, 'for a piece of exercise equipment that you don't even have to fold away. It just comes through the post and goes straight under the bed. We're calling it the plankerciser. It's a sure-fire winner. You can sell those suckers anything. We're awash with money.'

'So am I,' agreed a corporate executive in a shock revelation. 'I've got the stuff to burn. It's ridiculous. There's no way I can justify my salary. Every time I look at my pay cheque I just burst out laughing. And as for my automatic bonus – well, words fail me. Surely one day someone's got to realise I'm just a pretty ordinary guy working reasonably hard and that most of my work is straightforward stuff. No one's worth as much dosh as I get.'

In response to questioning he admitted that the gross increase in executive salaries over recent years had begun in the States. 'It's just greed,' he said, in a shock revelation, 'but I guess when you're near the top of the tree there's no one to stop you picking as many peanuts as you fancy.'

When informed that peanuts grew underground he laughed. 'Just goes to show I'm not the sharpest pencil in the box,' he said in a shock revelation. 'But I reckon you get away with what you can.'

'Hear, hear,' said a herbalist. 'I mean,' he added in a shock revelation, 'as far as I'm concerned the term herbal remedy is basically an oxymoron. Most illnesses come and go of their own accord, and we herbalists more or less rely on that. But if you contract one of the big nasties that won't go away, you're a damn fool if you take yourself off to the herb garden. You've got as much chance of finding a herbal cure as you have of hearing George Bush admit he screwed up.'

'I screwed up,' said George Bush in a shock revelation.

Ooooh la bloody la

'I think,' gushed the woman on the radio in a manner that immediately caused me to doubt the accuracy of the verb, 'I think that
France is such a wonderful sensory overload, don't you?'

'No,' I squealed, reaching for the volume control on the radio
with a vigour that almost broke the thing off, 'no, I bloody well
don't.'

How have the French done it? How have they hoodwinked the
world?

Well, let's start where the French start, and where they go on,
and where they also finish, which is with food. They are besotted
with food, and by and large they cook well. But boy, are they smug
about it. Smug and patronising and monomaniac. They are particularly boring about their regional delicacies – the terrine here, the
sucking pig there, and, in the region of France where I used to live,
the eau de vie de mirabelle. Eau de vie de mirabelle is a liqueur
made by infusing the flavours from the small and bitter local plum,
the mirabelle, into four-star petrol. The locals talked about it a lot
more than they drank it. They also gave it away in tellingly large
quantities.

The gushy woman on the radio no doubt finds France a sensory overload because they have outdoor markets where the women sniff melons, squeeze peaches, prod cheeses and generally go to enormous trouble to pass bacteria around. All of which is very picturesque in a touristy sort of way but for one thing it is not unique to France and for another thing I fail to see how it has contributed to the French image of romantic elegance.

For this I suspect we have to look at the language. French, they say, is the language of love. What they mean is that English is the language of love when spoken with a French accent. Why else should all French crooners – from Charles poloneck-sweater Aznavour to that ancient monsieur whose name I've forgotten but who used to knock 'em out with the highly suspect 'Zank heaven for leetle girls' – sing in English? When a Frenchman lays it on, rolling his r's, mispronouncing his th's and throwing the stress onto all ze wrong syllables, every English-speaking woman in a hundred-yard radius goes googly at the knee and subsides into a form of catatonia that disqualifies her from recognising that the average Frenchman is about as romantic as a diesel mechanic from Greymouth.

French itself is a heavily bastardised form of Latin, less mellifluous than Italian, less racy than Spanish and infinitely, but infinitely, less flexible than English. Hence the crusty Académie française is so terrified of the superior language that for years it has forbidden its citizens, on pain of being pelted to death with petanque balls, to say le weekend. The French, in an unusual display of wisdom, have ignored it.

There is no English Academy. Confident of its own resilience, English has cheerfully absorbed words from wherever it could get them and many have been French. And a remarkable number of these – chic, couture, suave – are associated with style rather than substance.

For somehow the land of berets, bicycles, onions, blue boiler suits, grey plaster houses with grey wooden shutters, straight roads, elm trees that may on reflection be poplars, too many poodles, throat-peeling cigarettes, feeble mopeds and thin beer into which they tip the nauseatingly sweet syrop de grenadine, has become a byword for style and fashion. And as for the notion that the women of France are supposed to be the most beautiful in the world, that stands up to the rigours of close inspection about as well as the notion that it is possible to play rugby against their menfolk without danger to one's testicles.

And then there's Paris. Paris, where fraudulent painters knock up daubs of Montmartre to flog to the tourist dupes and where the most famous building is a giant electricity pylon serving no practical purpose and which was erected in the late nineteenth century as a temporary bit of engineering show-offery. Constantly lauded as the most beautiful city of the world, the city of romance and all the rest of that guff, Paris, like every other European capital, has a fair collection of public buildings – emphatically excluding the Pompidou Centre – but some of the ugliest suburbs in the world, all high-rise sixties monstrosities and streets as mean as Miami.

Yet despite all this, despite the *Rainbow Warrior* and Moruroa Atoll, despite their embarrassing military and imperial record, despite the 2CV and the force-fed geese and the wines that aren't as good as ours, and despite in particular their extraordinary chauvinism – a word derived inevitably from a Frenchman, a Nicolas Chauvin who was ferociously patriotic and devoted in an unhealthy way to that bellicose dwarf Napoleon – France and the French retain a sort of mystique in the Anglo-Saxon mind. Off goes Peter Mayle to Provence to – God, I can hardly bring myself to type this – to do up a farmhouse, and his book sells a squillion copies.

The French are just people like everybody else. They have faults, they have virtues, they have a huge number of myths associated with them and they have a popular fizzy drink called Pshitt.

Wrong room

Last week I stayed in a expensive hotel. Someone else was paying.

The woman at reception programmed a credit card and called it my key. She also gave me a sachet of ground coffee.

On the wall in the lift a picture of a couple in the hotel dining room. She was all blouse and breast. His jaw jutted. Each had a plate of prawns, a glass of white wine and a smile as wide as a bridge.

In the corridor, Muzak, deep carpet and a row of doors like closed eyes. Behind them, no doubt, happy couples preparing to dine. Maids of foreign birth towed carts of sheets and soap and cleaning fluids, and flattened themselves against the wall as I approached.

It didn't take long to open my door with the credit card but the lights in the room didn't work. Because the lights didn't work I couldn't read the telephone instructions. I dialled 1 and spoke to a humming sound. I dialled 9 and spoke to silence. I dialled 0 and spoke to reception.

No, she said in a professional tone that made me feel foolish, of course I wasn't foolish.

When I slipped the credit card into the slot by the door the lights revealed a single chocolate at the head of the bed. While I ate it I read the note from the manager. It wished me happiness and used my Christian name. In search of happiness I opened every cupboard then dialled 0.

No, she said, there wasn't an ashtray because it wasn't a smoking room, and no of course she didn't think me foolish. I agreed to change rooms but didn't mention that I'd eaten the chocolate.

My new room was identical except for an ozone-maker – a metal cube with dials, like the sort of machine that you are supposed to but don't attach to the electricity supply when you're using a hedge trimmer in the rain.

I had to fill the kettle in the bathroom. It fitted awkwardly under the tap. I mopped the floor with two white towels and left them there.

A hotel room is the bed. I took the coffee plunger to the bed, wrestled the pillows from the counterpane, stacked them and folded the top one to support my neck. The bed was aligned inescapably to the television. I flicked through fifteen channels then watched golf. The players wore the same sort of clothes as the jut-jawed man who dined. The caddies wore bibs, like maids.

I would have liked a snack from the mini-bar – peanuts, biscuits, chocolate – but was scared of the prices. At the golf it started raining. The caddies held umbrellas over the players but not over themselves. I pressed the top of the coffee plunger. Coffee spurted over the bedside table and the ozone-maker. I rolled off the bed and fetched a towel from the bathroom then sat on the side of the bed and drank the coffee.

Putting the ironing board up to iron my shirt for the evening was easy. Putting it down again was beyond me. Choosing not to dial 0 I left the ironing board standing.

The bathroom was all mirrors and unguents. Tiny bottles of body lotion and moisturising cream and conditioner and two cakes of pomegranate and honey soap.

Getting the temperature right in the shower took only a few minutes, then I conditioned my armpits and moisturised my crotch. I hadn't closed the shower door properly. I dropped another towel on the floor to soak. While I was drying myself I wiped the condensation from the enormous mirror and did Mr Muscle poses.

I dressed, edged past the ironing board and went out.

I woke in the morning to knocking. A maid, breakfast and a newspaper. I ate in bed, spilling peach juice on my chest and yoghurt on the pillow. I licked the yoghurt off but couldn't reach the peach juice with my tongue. The countless sections of the unfamiliar newspaper dispersed themselves about the bed. On the television, highlights of the golf.

I showered again, using the last of the thousand towels, dressed, gathered my things, made to leave, stopped and surveyed the room that had been home for some fourteen hours. Sodden towels in the bathroom, the bed a stained shambles, the pillows piled haphazardly, the counterpane twisted like a bowel, the breakfast tray lying at a precarious angle, newspaper scattered, the ashtray full, coffee stains on the ozone-maker, the ironing board standing sentinel. Though the place cost $170 a night and was crammed with luxury, it and I had never found a fit. My chin never jutted. I never sipped the white wine, never peeled the prawns of pleasure.

In the corridor the self-effacing maids were hovering, waiting for me to go, waiting to put things right.

Hope is dead

Shoot the astrologers. Burn the tarot cards. I'll give you a glimpse round time's corner myself.

No need even to cross my palm with low-denomination banknotes – though a little gin money is always welcome in this cruel weather. Behold, for nothing, courtesy of my generous disposition, the future.

But before you behold, beware. It is dangerous to know the future. All who've peeped at it – Oedipus, Faust and many another sadsack – have come to ends so sticky you could mend furniture with them. Better to turn the page now. Stay ignorant and happy.

If you choose to keep reading, the risk is yours. You've been warned. And if, on some distant morning, you wake to foam-rubber decor and electrodes on your temples, well, don't come bleating to me.

Soppy to the core, we imagine the future will be nice. The future means winning the jackpot of happiness. The future means chance encounters with beautiful strangers who immediately stop being strangers and take their clothes off. Experience tells a different story, of course, but we all prefer the fantasies of hope.

Well, hope is dead. Take my hand and I will show you the way the world is going.

I have a friend whom I'll call Adam. He works for the government. Adam has recently been posted to a Pacific Island. And there, despite the twanging ukuleles and the languorous lagoons and the soporific heat and the feathery palms and the phosphorescent fish, Adam chooses not to lounge on the beach sipping drinks with umbrellas in. He goes running. The lounging locals stare at Adam with the sort of detached amusement with which Elizabethans stared at the mad.

Wild dogs infest the island. They stare at Adam with a less detached amusement. Apparently these dogs live on crabs. And the dogs see Adam as a dietary supplement. Adam is understandably alarmed. Knowing I know something of dogs, Adam sought my advice.

I wrote Adam a substantial email. I told him of a Victorian vicar who always carried a coat and an umbrella. If a bad dog approached, the vicar draped the coat over the umbrella and shoved it at the dog. The dog seized the coat. This positioned the dog nicely for the vicar to swing his boot and collect the dog under the chin. Ungodly but effective.

I wrote plenty more such helpful stuff, including a cheerful description of a removal man I once saw bitten on the buttocks by a dog. Then I pressed 'send'. But the email did not reach Adam. The government sent it back to me.

For all I know, at this very moment and for want of my advice, Adam may be down on the sand beside the languorous lagoon being mauled to death by wild dogs, while the locals look on with detached amusement, strumming their ukuleles and taking care not to stab themselves in the eye with a drink umbrella. If so, blame the government. Or more specifically, blame MailMarshal.

Because MailMarshal intercepted my email to Adam, read it, went puce around the gills, and sent it back with a note attached. It was a curt note. No 'dear' at the start. No parting benison of love or kisses.

Here is what Mailmarshal wrote:

MailMarshal (an automated content monitoring gateway) has stopped the email for the following reason:

It believes it may contain unacceptable language, or inappropriate material.

Please remove any inappropriate language and send it again.

Script Offensive Material Triggered

Expression: (my OR your OR nice OR big OR the OR her OR his OR fat OR tight OR sweet OR great) FOLLOWED BY 'arse'

And there we have it. Behold tomorrow in all its unglory. Told off by a machine. A machine, furthermore, that is not subject to its own rules. I sent it a mild vulgarity. It sent me back a note so suggestive, so crammed with boggling sexual possibility, that I had to lie down and fan myself with a dog-eared copy of the *Norwegian Naturist*.

Once I'd recovered I set to work on MailMarshal. To find out where it drew its lines, I sent it screeds of emails. It accepted gluteus maximus. It accepted bum, buttocks, bottom, situpon, posterior, rectum and jacksie. But it turned down, well, let's not worry about what it turned down.

In a final provocative torrent I sent Mailmarshal a note using every one of the offending words it sent me, and more than a few of my own, a note so rich that it would have shivered the timbers of my nautical great-uncle Dick. MailMarshal has yet to reply.

But it will. Machines persist. They know no better. MailMarshal will carry on long after the death of the prurient bureaucrat who programmed it. Indeed, long after Adam's bones have been bleached to the colour of the sand they may be lying on, long after Baghdad has been razed to rubble, long after, indeed, the human race has poisoned or bombed itself into holes in the ground, MailMarshal, son of MailMarshal, and a host of other 'content monitoring gateways' will be protecting us from naughty words, imposing arbitrary illiterate primness on words sent from friend to friend.

Automated censorship. You read it here first.

No children litter the step

In sepia snaps of early nineteenth-century New Zealand, settlements consist of wooden shacks with corrugated roofs and sprawls of dusty grinning urchins in the street outside. But in among the fragile penetrable buildings stand two more solid ones of brick or masonry, like sound teeth in a rotting mouth. One's the church. The other is a four-square double-storey thing. Its windows are small and grilled, its title etched in plaster round the pediment. Its doors are flanked by Graeco-Roman columns. No children litter its step. It is the bank.

Banks do simple business. They borrow money at a certain rate and lend it at another. The difference between the two buys window-grilles and plaster pediments and suits as dull as Sunday.

Banks are adult. Banks are sober. Banks are austere. And banks are necessary. We hold them in our minds, as we do most authorities, in double guise. We depend on them and yet we like to dislike them.

Few children aspire to banking. It doesn't cut a dash. It is the embodiment of prudence. Prudence, said Blake, is a rich, ugly, old maid courted by incapacity. But banks are capable.

Inactive things themselves, they put their money out to people who are active, people who will do and make things. In exchange banks take a slice of profit. Effectively banks gamble. Admittedly they gamble on as close to racing certainties as they can find, but a punt remains a punt. Yet though we love a punter, it's hard to love a bank.

Banks call their services products, but they lie. They produce nothing but profits. They trade in money and money is not a thing in itself, but rather a medium, an image of things. You can't eat it. You can't build or hunt or grow things with it. You can't fight with it. Take a million bucks into the bush and see what it's worth. It makes reasonable but short-lived kindling.

We feel ambiguously towards money. We love the stuff because of its wad-weight of promise, the potential for delight that it holds within its sexy numbers. But we also despise it. We talk of being filthy rich. We talk of rolling in it. Money has a strange totemic quality, a religious aura. We are shy of openly discussing it. We speak of it in euphemisms, just as we do of God or sex. Money becomes funds, revenue streams, allocations.

That same ambivalence extends to banks. Though most of us choose to use a bank and readily accept the interest that it pays, and the loan that it extends to help us buy a house, we universally resent the fees it charges for the work it does, and the way that it protects itself from loss. We see it somehow as a parasite upon our industry. And we resent it as we resent anything to which we are indebted.

We don't like bank robbers but only because they terrify the workers. We don't feel sorry for the bank itself. If you prick a bank it doesn't bleed. And let some years elapse and bank robbers can metamorphose into heroes. Ned Kelly now is Robin Hood. And

Nick Leeson, who brought down the Barings Bank by speculating psychopathically, does not seem like a villain. A fool perhaps, a wild man sunk by greed, but not a villain.

Yet still, despite the grumbles and resentment, the mutterings of impotence, our comfort rests on banks. A run on the banks knocks struts from underneath our lives and makes us scared.

Banks are patriarchal figures, like serious remote Victorian fathers. We kick against them but we want them there. They underpin, they represent security.

Modern bankers understand all this. And in a bid to generate more business they strive to make us feel more warmth towards them. Their ads cry out for love. They paint themselves as donors of freedom. Come bank with us and you will paraglide to happiness. Come bank with us and you'll be stallion-free. Come bank with us and you will meet a very funny man.

But like advertisers everywhere they paint in bogus colours. Inside even the most open-plan and customer-friendly banks, the atmosphere is never playful, never funny, never free. It is austere and serious and churchlike. The queue is often silent as in church. Each customer goes to the counter as if to the confessional. Each conversation's private. And however much the teller-priest may smile and talk of weather or of sport, the conversation's nothing more than froth. Behind it, like the fat-doored safe behind the teller, there stands the iron-bound moral law of sums. And sins against that law are printed, as they've always been, in scarlet.

Hot wet air

From the twenty-first floor of the Excelsior Hotel I can see the mouth of the Singapore River. Beyond it in the open sea a massive fleet of cargo ships lies at anchor. This place was built on trade.

Near the water's edge a group of boys plays soccer. I don't know how they can. Singapore sits smack on the equator. The air's like a wet oven.

To one side stands the spire of the Cathedral of St Andrew. I went there yesterday. The place had all the bits that make a Western church – vaulted ceiling, stone columns, brass eagle lectern, font and organ, pew backs crammed with hymnbooks – but it was hot. The twenty hanging electric fans did nothing but stir the heat. Seated on a wickerwork pew I felt no relief from the city. My trousers were sodden at the crotch. Skin stuck to cloth, to skin. There was hot wet grit in my armpits, in the creases of my neck.

The church seemed like what it is, a transplant from the cool north, ill-suited to the globe's sweltering girdle. High up on the west wall of the church, something jungle-luxuriant sprouted from the spouting. You could see it getting bigger.

The church doesn't fit here. Nor do white people. We are too lardy and large. In the hotel lobby, Australian women in late middle age with truck-tyre waists and bangled flabby arms are loud and crass. I wince at our shared heritage. And yet Singapore is endlessly polite to us. It takes our bags and pampers us with yes-sir, no-sir. The air-conditioning and courtesy invite us just to spend.

Two centuries ago it was not so. Up empty Canning Rise there is an imitation of a European park. The grass is coarse and broad of leaf and the soil is sand, but there are band rotundas and benches under trees, and there I found the tombstones of some European dead. In 1863 a sailor born in Telpham, Sussex, died aged twenty-one. The tropics took him, raddled him no doubt with some extravagant disease that blew him up or shrank him, turned his young flesh purple, shook his teeth out, killed him. His shipmates all chipped in to build his tomb. The tropics got that too. The tomb caved in. Only the headstone survived to be bricked into a wall.

Nearby stands the Wesleyan church. An information board boasts the evangelical history of the place. Hot wet air has crept behind the glass to make most of the boast illegible.

Some fifty cranes are clustered on a building site. Signs announce the construction of the Singapore Institute of Management, with posters of happy students doing handstands. The workmen on the site are skinny, muscled and dark, their chocolate eyes set deep in the head. I can only guess at their race. This is a city of many races. There are tiny Chinese girls, turbaned Sikhs, broad-faced Malays and probably a hundred other Asian races I can't discriminate. If there is an indigenous population, I don't know what it is. And the heat makes me incurious.

As everybody knows, Singapore is orderly. There is no chewing gum. Nor, in the centre of the city at least, are there beggars or litter. Those who would be begging are employed to sweep the streets. Each carries a worn broom and a plastic pan on a stick.

The hand of authority lies heavily on the place. Inside the buildings a hundred thousand signs say 'No Smoking – By Law'. Unnecessary security guards stand sentry outside shops and hotels. No hawkers pester me. Everyone obeys the pedestrian lights. A blinking numeral counts down the seconds left to me to cross the road. I take them all.

Shopping malls abound, cool and multi-storeyed, neon-lit and primary-coloured, open late into the night. In Raffles City Shopping Plaza there is Marks & Spencer, and Aunt Jodie's coffee bar. The ground floor holds a temporary exhibition of Australian produce. Yesterday, among the people picking over merino woollen clothes, boxed Tasmanian honeycombs and glassware painted by authentic Aborigines, were quite a few Australians.

In the Raffles City Shopping Plaza Food Mart I drank a mango smoothie and ate five dollars worth of noodles topped with duck. The duck was mostly bone. To smoke I had to go outside. On a low wall by a carpark I sat and wrote some notes. The ballpoint ink took time to dry. The moisture had nowhere to go. Under a hedge trimmed military square a fat rat nosed for rubbish and found none.

This morning, with time to kill before my taxi to the airport, I make a final sortie out into the heat. In the hotel forecourt I ask a man in uniform to tell me somewhere good for breakfast.

'Madonna,' he says, and points along the street.

'Madonna?'

'Madonna,' he repeats and smiles. 'Good,' he says. 'American.'

I cotton on and smile back. 'No,' I say, 'not McDonald's. Is there somewhere more, well, more Singaporean?'

'Singaporean?' he says.

I nod. He smiles and shrugs.

I thank him and trudge away. My feet are swollen. It's not the place's fault, but I'll be pleased to leave. I don't belong.

Easter rising

Easter Sunday, Hitler's birthday, mine too, as it happens, and this morning saw the resurrection of Grandma Chook, which is as good a birthday present as I've had since the pair of handcuffs. To be frank, Grandma Chook wasn't actually dead, but I thought she was, which if you think about it, and I did, is worse. I mean, if you're not dead but people think you are, and they're rootling in the cupboard for something to wear to your funeral and a few words to say about you that aren't actively malicious, it's no time to pop back up saying, 'Yoohoo, it's me, yes, that's right, I was just foxing, God what a horrible suit.' No, you're better off out of it.

Which is what I thought Grandma Chook was, only I couldn't find the corpse. She disappeared on whatever they call the day before Good Friday – Okay Thursday, perhaps – and no hint of her since.

She was a callous old matriarch, much given to bullying the other chooks, all of whom are her daughters or granddaughters. Having ruled the roost for half a decade she had grown monstrously fat, far too fat to even think of flying, too fat indeed to hop up a 1-foot retaining wall that I built and which is still, remarkably, retaining. So fat was Grandma Chook that whenever I appeared at the back door and she came barrelling down the slope with her greed and fluffy underskirts to ensure she was first to bury her beak in the trough, gravity regularly took her a couple of yards past the target and dumped her in a feathery heap against the fence with her multiple offspring all trying hard not to giggle.

But then, suddenly, on Okay Thursday, there she was, gone. I checked her usual roosting sites, I checked the nesting box where she retires twice a year to brood, I fossicked through the undergrowth like a police search party of one, but zilch, zip, nothing, only a hole where she'd been. And to my surprise I missed her. I missed her bossy clucking selfish vigour, and it didn't make for a very Good Friday. Nor, for that matter, a Super Saturday, especially when added to the antics of the Post Office.

Did you get one of those billets doux from New Zealand Post? Dear Householder and Victim, it said, we've decided to give our coochy-coo postie-wosties an extra day off on Super Saturday so they can have a really jolly time at Easter with their kiddiwinkies and you can have virtually a whole week without mail. Please use this card to tell us whether you think this is a good idea, even though we're going to do it anyway, or whether you think we should keep our postie-wosties working every hour that God gives until they are skeletal husks fit only for paupers' graves.

Naturally I wrote back. Whip 'em to death, I wrote, in red ink and capital letters, but it won't make any difference. Not that it matters, I suppose, since no one writes letters any more and all the postie ever brings me is illiteracies from real estatists, and supermarket fliers telling me how cheaply I can buy a dead chook, which, frankly, was not what I needed right then.

What I needed right then on Super Saturday, with a pall of

gloom, loss and solitude descending, was available at the Lava Bar for four dollars a pint. Down the evening hill I toddled with the slightly less than full moon squatting above the plantation ridge like a giant egg. Never – and when I say never, I mean not all that often – have I seen the moon looking more egglike, which, as I said straight off to the barman, was singularly apt for Easter. That, inevitably, led to a grand discussion of the etymology of the word Easter, which I said went back to some pagan festival called Oestre that the church hijacked, as is its habit, and the barman said was it related to oestrogen, that being something to do with eggs and fertility, to which I said with resonant conviction that I hadn't got a clue. I went on to lament the fate of Grandma Chook and everyone said how sad they were, which was about as convincing as a party political broadcast, and then the evening ended in the not so small hours in a bizarre escapade with someone else's dog which was jolly while it lasted.

So ten seconds or so after waking on Easter Sunday I realised I was unwell and forty-six for the first time in my life. I stumbled out to feed the chooks and from under the house there came a huffing and a clucking and a flapping of elderly wings and out waddled Grandma Chook. She was famished. I watched her eat a bushel or two of grain and then followed her back under the house where somehow she had amassed a clutch of twenty eggs, all of them infertile, which she was spending her Easter holidays trying to hatch. And as I reached under her to remove the eggs – because if I didn't she would sit on them till Easter next – she pecked my hand with what I can only describe as undisguised and entirely typical malice. Welcome back from the dead, I said, and I meant it.

How to be happy

Take your dog with you on holiday. Dogs love holidays and are good at them. They also love you and hate kennels. Furthermore, if you do take your dog with you, you will add to the sum of happiness in the world. And if those aren't reasons enough to convince you, then you are sick.

You don't have to wait for a dog to pack. A dog is always packed. It's got its collar on and it won't sulk if you forget the lead.

Dogs rarely throw up in the car. And if they do, they eat it back up. Nor do dogs squabble in the car. They just stick their heads out of the window and are happy. They like ice creams, but they don't whine for them. And they never ask if you're nearly there yet. Dogs think you're already there, because, for a dog, there is here, and here is the best possible place to be. In five minutes time the best possible place to be will be where you are in five minutes time. But dogs don't know that until they get there, because they have no command of the future tense.

Dogs don't mind if you go to the same place every year. Nor do they hanker for abroad in the belief that abroad is better. They don't imagine that if they go abroad they will somehow become more adventurous. A dog knows that wherever it goes it will just be the same old dog, and it is happy with that.

A dog doesn't ask if its bum looks big in this. A dog hasn't got a this for its bum to look big in. Nor has it got a big bum.

Dogs admire the way you barbecue. They will watch you barbecue for hours. If you burn all the meat you can hide it inside the dog. After the barbecue you can lay the cooled griddle on the ground. It will be clean in the morning.

Having a dog on holiday will excuse you from guided tours, craft galleries, souvenir shops and other places where you would spend money on stuff you don't want. Dogs don't want you to buy stuff you don't want. Dogs want you to play. Playing is better for you than buying stuff.

Because you have spent the year watching sport on television you will have forgotten how to play beach cricket. The dog will remind you. When you are trying very hard to win, the dog will pick up the ball and run into the sea. You will swear at the dog and chase it and then you will give up, stand still, look at the sky and laugh. Then you will say 'Thank you, dog, for reminding me how to play beach cricket.'

Dogs will help you meet people. Some people will say 'What a nice dog' and 'How old is your nice dog?' and 'What's your nice dog called?' These people are good people. If you are single you may have sex with some of these people. If you are not single, you can imagine having sex with all of these people. If you imagine having sex with them, the dog won't know. If you do have sex with them, the dog won't mind. Though it will want to join in.

You will also meet people who bunch their eyebrows and swear and say 'That dog should be on a lead'. These are sad people. They have become infected by fear and by the media and they have forgotten how to find happiness, and in particular how to find happiness in the happiness of others. Have nothing to do with these killjoys until after midnight. After midnight, go out and let their tents down. Take the dog with you.

When the killjoys are writhing and squealing under the canvas, the dog will think it's a game. Encourage the dog to join the game, then go back to your tent. The dog will come home eventually. The killjoys will go home in the morning. You can then move your tent to the killjoys' camping site because it is better than yours. The dog will be as happy in the new camping site as it was in the old camping site as it is in any camping site.

In sum, then, the best way to enjoy a holiday is to imitate your dog. Wear as little as possible. Presume people are nice until you find out otherwise. When something is going on, join in. When nothing is going on, sleep.

But it is hard to imitate a dog that isn't there. Take the dog with you. Everyone will be happy.

Lucy mon

Oh golly gosh, I'm having trouble with my eyboard. The letter ' ' seems to have got stuc.

I found this out when I sent an email to Andy and he wrote back instanter saying 'What's a mon?' I wrote back saying 'mon' was a form of address in Scotland, normally preceded, for reasons that eluded me, by 'hoots'. 'Fair enough,' wrote Andy, 'but why are you living the life of one?', which puzzled me a bit until I had a pee at my previous email.

'Sorry,' I wrote immediately, 'having problems with the letter ' '. Didn't mean mon, but rather mon, you now, one of those religious chaps that lives in a convent', and Andy wrote back 'Don't you mean monastery?' to which I replied, 'Not if he's a lucy mon, I don't.'

I touch-type of course. It would be unprofessional not to. But I loo at the eyboard at the same time, because one can't be too sure in this precarious world. Belt and braces, that's the way to go. And besides, how else am I supposed to now where the letters are?

The consequence is, of course, that I don't loo at the screen, and I fire off emails to Andy with no ' 's in them. As soon as he pointed out the problem, I tried pressing the k. I pressed it again and again and again. Once or twice it worked (see), but generally not a dicy bird.

In one way it was great fun. It threw up all sort of strangenesses that refreshed, I felt, the tired old language. 'Dicy bird', for example, brings to mind the great Condor of Fortune that once soared above the Andes. The Aztecs sacrificed ids to it in the hope that it would bless them with the shelter of its wings, instead of dumping on them from high in the sy.

And the missing ' ' breathed fresh life into old joes.

Patient: 'Doctor, doctor, I thin I'm a leptomaniac.'

Doctor: 'Have you taen anything for it?'

The missing ' ' could have altered the course of history. 'iss me, Hardy,' says the dying Nelson, to which Hardy replies, 'Of course iss you. Who did you thin I thought it was?'

'No,' groans Nelson in extremis, 'I meant "iss me". Iss me now, Hardy, before it's too late. Please.'

'Shoot him, Lieutenant,' says Hardy. 'We can't let the crew see him lie this. He's gone completely boners.'

(Of course one can programme a computer to do fun stuff automatically. I sometimes amuse myself – it's a lonely life being a hac columnist – by telling the machine to replace the letter 'e' with something infantile like 'bottom' and then I typbottom a linbottom or two for fun, though I admit that it soon grows a bit tirbottom-sombottom.)

Anyway, I suppose things could be worse. Imagine if I was writing a novel and I also lost the letter ' ', number four in the blooy alphabet, and I ha a main character in the novel whose name was ic. It would mae life very har inee.

I have got a 'd', fortunately, but the ' ' really has got stuc, and though, as I say, it is fun in one way, it is also disastrous. Because when I told Andy that I'd been living the life of a mon I was speaing the truth. I've been monish because I'm writing a boo. It isn't a novel about Dic, but it is 85,000 words long and it's due at the publisher in four days. I'll get there, I thin, just, but it's been tough. I actually haven't had a drin for twenty-seven days, which is, I believe, the longest drought since about 1971. The liver thins it's in clover – though in four days time it's in for one hell of a shoc.

But with the polishing still to be done to the text I've now got a problem. It's all very well to write a column with no ' 's in it, but I can hardly whac this sort of thing off to the publisher. Should I just eep on eeping on, and try to sirt round all the words with ' 's in them, or should I try to fix the eyboard? And if I try to fix the eyboard, what if it all goes wrong and I only compound the problem. I've got this really trendy computer that won't tae a dis, so I can't mae a copy of the text. I could lose the lot. Six months wor up in smoe.

But I've got this little aerosol of stuff that advertises itself as 'the toolbox in a can' and perhaps if I just give the letter ' ' a teensy-weensy squirt, lie so

At the Dickens

I'd always wanted to get into motivational speaking but I owe the chance to my Auntie Debs. When she finally fell off the poop deck after a long and lucrative career in the fishing industry I was her sole heir. My brother got the cod.

But neither of us was interested in fishing. He sold his cod immediately and I palmed off my sole to a nice little man with a beard and a fork. We were rich. My brother was a born idler and took off for the land of milk and honey. But I stayed put.

For years, you see, I'd had my ear to the ground and my nose to the wind. As a result I had my eye on a struggling little motivational speakers' bureau in town. It was called the Dickens and had fallen on hard times.

On a breezy March morning I strode into the Dickens clutching my fishing cheque. I pushed open the battered door and found myself in a deep and fusty gloom. The place was scattered with dusty accoutrements. The Dickens was one bleak house.

As my pupils widened in the crepuscular office I made out a figure slumped over the only desk. I pulled out a gin bottle and he came to with a jerk. Pausing only to tell the jerk to beat it, I poured us both a stiff one and came straight to the point.

'Mr Dickens,' I said, 'I hear you got motivational speakers.'

He laughed a laugh so hollow that I tipped my slug of gin into it. 'Mate,' he said, 'I got more motivational speakers than you can shake a stick at.' He handed me a stick.

I shook it. And suddenly the dusty accoutrements took shape as human figures, shambling and derelict, score upon score of them. I tried to shake my stick at all of them but there were too many.

'How much for the lot?' I asked.

'Yours for a song.'

I gave him a Christmas carol and he was out the door of the Dickens before you could say knife.

'Knife,' said one of the shambling figures.

'Too late,' I said, 'he's gone. You're mine now. Now get out there and get motivating.'

'Ha,' said the shambling figure. 'You greenhorn. Any idea how many motivational speakers there are these days? The country's swarming with them. Ex-alcoholics, buggered triathletes, slimming champions, swimming champions, positive thinkers, stockmarket gurus – billions of us. And no one wants to hear us any more. People have seen through us. Everyone I know in the industry is trying to get out of it.'

Before you could say Jack Robinson I realised what I had to do. I buttonholed the shambling speaker. 'Name?' I barked.

'Jack Robinson,' he said.

'Jack,' I cried, 'we have nothing to fear but fear itself. I'm going to release your creative energies in a way that you wouldn't have dared to dream possible. Are you with me, Jack?'

'Whatever,' said Jack gloomily, 'but I never was into that positive thinking caper. I was the super-memory man. You know, twenty tapes for three easy payments of $99, guaranteed to help you recall everyone's name at a party.'

'Yeah, yeah,' I said, 'what happened to that racket?'

'Don't remember,' said Jack, 'but it's dead now, like everything else in this biz.'

'He's right,' came a voice, 'you don't have to be a rocket scientist to see it's all over, mate. They've rumbled us.'

'Name?'

'Kuzolski. Rocket scientist. Chief safety engineer on the Voyager mission.

'The one they lost touch with?'

'No, the one that blew up 'cause of a cock-up by the chief safety engineer. When NASA gave me the elbow I thought I'd try the motivational speaking line. "'Your mistakes are your biggest asset' by the man who blew up the space probe." Thought it would be a nice comfy little number, you know, regular pay cheque, no responsibilities, all that stuff. And look at me now. Look at all of us.' He gestured to his fellow motivators, slumped in the shadows. 'We're dog tucker, mate, yesterday's men. No one's swallowing our baloney any more. Unleash your creative potential, be the CEO of your self, every idea's a good idea.' He chuckled. 'That particular idea was probably the worst of the lot.'

A murmur of assent scurried through the ranks.

'So,' I said, 'if motivation's a goner, where do we go from here?'

'Demotivation?' said one wag, from the echoing depths of his gloom.

'Precisely,' I bellowed. 'Got it in one.' I sensed eyes flicker into life and look up at me.

'It's time,' I said, 'to rediscover the wisdom of the ancients. Delude yourself is out. Know thyself's back in.'

I looked at my congregation of demotivated motivators. An old familiar light was burning in their eyes. One by one their careworn faces were shaking off their looks of rusty depression and shining like new roofing iron. They were galvanised.

'Now, put your little thinking caps on. I want ideas. I want catchphrases. I want mottos.'

'How about,' said Jack, '"Dare to be ordinary"?'

'Be alive. Work nine to five.'

'Orville Wright was wrong.'

'Stay at work. You're just a jerk.'

I've no need to go on. You're familiar with the story. How the Dickens Academy of Demotivation blew the whole motivational speaker racket out the water. Made people happy to be who they were. Put all the team-building confidence courses into bankruptcy. To cut a long story short, I made a killing, cashed up at the peak of the market and flew out to join my bro in the land of milk and honey.

But things had turned sour for him. He'd come to a sticky end.

Playing with god

'Are you saved?' he asked.

We are supposed to live and learn. And if there is one thing I have learned from living it is to ignore people who ask me if I'm saved. It's a poor question at the best of times, and this wasn't the best of times. I was playing the man at chess.

I've joined an internet chess club. It's lovely. At any hour I can press 'seek' on my computer. This sends a tug down one tiny filament of the World Wide Web and somewhere in cyberspace a chess enthusiast will tug back. It can be anyone from an idle Indonesian to a Lapp at a loose end. A virtual chessboard appears before the pair of us, we agree on the time limit of the game and we're away.

Sometimes your opponent sends you messages while you play: 'Greetings from Grimsville, Latvia' – that sort of thing. I reply with 'Lots of love from Lyttelton', and generally that's that. For chess is a consuming business. No more words are exchanged until someone's king lies prone, a bishop's dagger buried in its kidneys. Then the politely jubilant Latvian types 'Thanx, good game' and scuttles off to find a better one. But not so with this man. He blocked my opening pawn with a pawn, then asked me whether I was saved.

Chess is psychological. Distracting an opponent is good. Upsetting him is better.

'Didn't know that I was lost,' I typed, then nudged another pawn.

He moved his bishop, then 'Do you know Jesus?' he asked. I didn't like this man.

He wasn't really asking. Rather he was smugly implying not only that he was on first name terms with Jesus – no Mr Christ for him – and that he was therefore heading upstairs for an eternity of harps and strawberries, but also that he cared about me. He didn't care about me. He'd never met me and he never would. For all he knew I could be a computer. (Several chess computers lurk in cyberspace. I avoid them. They thrash me by never making mistakes. Playing a computer is like playing god.)

I shifted my knight. Out came his queen. Then 'Do you know Jesus?' he repeated.

'Who?' I typed.

That got him. His reply was instantaneous and curt. 'Go see *The Passion of the Christ*,' he wrote.

My clock was ticking. Time is as cruel in chess as in life. When the end is near and death crowds around your king, you can never regain seconds that you frittered when the game was young. Nor can you retract your errors. Every sin returns to bite you. The pawn you casually ceded at the start proves eighty-eight moves later to be just the piece you need to plug the gap through which the final mortal thrust is coming. In chess you pay. In chess there's no forgiveness. I pushed out a third pawn to threaten his bishop and stop my clock.

Then 'No,' I typed. 'I won't see *Passion of the Christ*. I've already seen a film by Mr Melville Gibson. It was called *Braveheart* and though I don't wish to seem rude, I thought, on balance, that it was perhaps the most appalling piece of cinematic trash that I have had the ill luck to lay eyes on in all my forty-seven years. It starred a cast of rural Scots in kilts, each with an aura of virtue that didn't quite tally with my experiences of Glasgow on a wet Wednesday in winter. Their rugged goodness, flinchless courage and porridge-fuelled honesty were underlined by panoramic shots of heather, lochs and glens and other barren tourist falsehoods underscored with bagpipes. Braveheart himself, a sort of Jesus character, made Mills and Boonish love on horseback to an authentic Scottish peasant wench from Santa Barbara whose thirteenth-century make-up never ran, not even when they carried on beneath a waterfall accompanied by an unseen orchestra of fifty sweeping violins.

'The English, on the other hand, all looked like gargoyles. The king was a snivelling paedophile, his soldiers torturers or rapists. The English never gathered in romantic heather, but rather in some dungeon underground where all was dank and treacherous. And obviously every time an Englishman appeared on screen the orchestra shut up.

'In short,' I typed, and by this time my fingers were thumping the keyboard, 'it was a lousy piece of propaganda, the corniest corn since cornflakes, and if you're suggesting that a film director capable of producing that sort of pap could . . .'

The computer made a noise. I looked up at the screen. 'Game over' it said. My opponent's queen was nestled beside my king and guarded by his bishop. The simplest shortest gambit in the book of chess. Fool's mate.

'Thanx, good game,' typed Mr Are-you-saved and went.

There are times you have to laugh. This was not one of those times. I pressed the button called 'seek'. I had a new opponent within seconds. 'Greetings from Düsseldorf,' he typed.

'Lots of love from Lyttelton,' I answered. 'Are you saved?'

You live and learn.

Warm, wet and threatless

I had a theory about the bathroom habits of the sexes, but I lacked evidence to support it. So I went to the trouble and expense of doing a survey. With full statistical rigour I surveyed everybody sitting at the bar.

The survey resoundingly proved my theory to be true: women prefer baths and men prefer showers. Or, to put it another way, my survey confirmed that men are more sensible than women, more hygienic, thrifty, musical and conscious of the dwindling of the earth's resources. I enjoyed typing that sentence. It will bring me death threats.

My theory may also explain why men are still in charge of most things. By the time a woman has run a bath, got the temperature right, soaked herself, soaped herself and played with her duck, a man has had a shower, put on a tie, gone to work and done at least half an hour of shouting. But what it doesn't explain is why women like baths so much.

The bath has a totemic quality. It often appears in television advertisements, containing a lot of bubbles and a woman stupefied with pleasure. That woman is not me.

Nevertheless I was brought up with a bath. I was dropped into it every second night along with my elder brother. And it was in that bath I learned that there is no sensation worse than water up the nostrils. It spells panic in capital letters. I was also suspicious of shampoo. It tasted bad and stung the eyes, so God alone knew what it was doing to my hair. Now I know that too. It was making my hair fall out.

When my brother decided he preferred to bath alone – a decision forced on him by the courses he chose at university – I had to run my own bath. I soon learned that the perfect temperature for a bath is the one it isn't at.

I also learned that the hand is a bad thermometer. Dangle it in a too-hot bath and it will tell you that it's not too hot, so you step in. Feet are better thermometers, but they are slow. You can stand there for several seconds while the too-hot message lumbers up the legs, circumnavigates the pelvis, dawdles up the spinal column and then emerges through the oesophagus as a yelp. You leap from the bath like a pole vaulter and find you've gained a pair of vermilion ankle socks.

So you cool the bath a little, before stepping back in. Then you grip the sides and lower your vulnerabilities towards the water in the manner of a tentative anglepoise lamp.

At this stage you hold your breath, so that at the moment of contact you can emit a series of little gasps like a chimp's orgasm. As you finally submerge your shoulders and the water sloshes lovingly onto the bathroom floor, you complete the chimp orgasm with a long satisfied 'aaaah'.

But then what? A chimp just says thanks, cleans itself up and goes about its business. But the bath-taker, well, what is there to for him to do? Lie there stewing in his own dirt? Constantly and inaccurately adjust the taps with his toes in an effort to keep the temperature right? Read a book? I've no idea. You'll have to ask a woman.

The only bath I remember liking was after rugby. Someone else filled it and both teams got into it. If you were the fifth team playing on a muddy day, the bath looked like a tourist attraction in Rotorua. But unlike a tourist attraction in Rotorua, you could smoke, drink beer and boast to twenty-nine other men in it.

These days I rarely bath with twenty-nine men. The last person I bathed with was Jane Austen. I'd bought a house that came with a salmon pink spa-bath studded with water jets in what looked like amusing locations. Eager to try it I plucked Jane from the shelves and stripped off. To make the jets jet there was a small electric motor conveniently housed just below my right shoulder. When I pressed the button to start it my eyes vibrated. So did Jane Austen. Sadly the eyes and Jane vibrated at different speeds. I gave up, got out and have never had a bath since.

But every woman I know has. Though showers are better than baths for all purposes, up to and including sex and opera, women persist in taking baths.

Why is this so? Relentless in pursuit of truth I put the question to all the women in my bar survey. 'What exactly is it,' I said to her, 'that you like about baths? Is it that they offer a refuge from a spiky world, a cocooning warmth and privacy, an escape from the demands of children and men? Or is it that you are fundamentally a tactile being and a bath is like a million warm and threatless hands exploring you? Or is it something Freudian, a journey of nostalgia to the womb, a floating in the waters of security, a reversion to an amniotic world?'

'Yeah,' she said. So now you know.

Lies to spare

Lies hold our world up. Take away the scaffolding of lies and things fall down. God, pornography, 100 per cent Pure New Zealand, deodorant, down they tumble. Rubble the lot. It's great fun.

Take mega-butch four-wheel drive recreational vehicles. I wish you would. I can't see round them, past them or under them. Monstrous things, rolling off the automated assembly lines in Nagoya and Seoul, to infest the world. They're built of lies, lies from here to my Aunt Fanny. Lies from bull bar (Oh, those poor shunted bulls. You have to go miles these days to find an unshunted one) to tailgate.

Let's look at the tailgate. I often have to. It blocks my windscreen. It's got a spare wheel stuck on it.

Small cars haven't got a spare wheel stuck on them. Minis find space for their spare wheels somewhere inside. Mega-butches don't. Though their cabin space is measured in hectares, there's no room for the spare.

A lie, of course. There's room to spare for the spare. But the spare is hung on the back for a reason. It's hung there to tell fibs. 'Look at me,' bellows the spare, 'I am rugged practicality. My owners wear safari suits with sweat stains in the armpits. My owners know the world's awash with peril. My owners can cope.'

The dangling spare tyre implies that the moment one of the other tyres is picked off by a sniper, or holed by an assegai, or shredded by a landmine in the badland wastes of the supermarket carpark, Mr or Mrs Safari-Armpit will leap from the cab, fall to their knees on the sun-bleached tarmac and make with the jack before you can say charging rhinoceros. They are rugged and practical people, men and women of action, terse, hard and with honest dirt beneath their fingernails. So says the spare.

But that isn't all it says. The spare tyre is shrouded in a tyre cover. That tyre cover prompts a question. That question is why?

The tyre cover can't be there to keep the tyre dry. Tyres don't mind getting wet.

And the tyre cover can't be there to protect the hands and clothing of Mr and Mrs Safari-Armpit. These are rugged people who care nothing for a smudge of dirt on the safari suit.

No, that tyre cover exists to send yet another lie out into the world to breed. The one I pootled along behind today told me a corker of a fib. And all in three words.

The first of these words was the name of the car-maker. Let's call it Carcorp. The other two words, in sequence, were 'likes' and 'nature'.

Carcorp likes nature. Well, isn't that just dandy.

Let's start with the first lie. Carcorp doesn't like nature. Carcorp doesn't like anything. It doesn't like cricket or pavlova or sex. It can't. It isn't a sentient being. It doesn't have feelings.

Carcorp is an organisation of lots of sentient beings, some of whom may like cricket, pavlova and sex, some of whom may even like them simultaneously, and some of whom may like none of them. But the only thing that binds these beings together is not what they like and dislike, but the making and selling of cars in order to earn dosh. Which is fine by me. I approve of cars. But not of fibs.

The purpose of saying 'Carcorp Likes Nature' is that we then think of Carcorp as a person, and a nice person at that. Carcorp is not going to publish a slogan such as 'Carcorp Kills Cats', even though it's a chunky, alliterative and memorable slogan. And a true one. Worldwide in the course of a normal day Carcorp probably runs over several tonnes of cats. But cat-slaughtering doesn't make Carcorp out to be a nice chap. No, Carcorp likes nature.

Nature here means cuddly things. It means soft grass and lapping waters and gentle herbivorous beasties that feed from our hands and look good on postcards.

If 'Carcorp Likes Nature' is true, then, by the rules of logic, the following statements must also be true. Carcorp likes blowflies. Carcorp likes warthogs. Carcorp likes death from exposure. Carcorp is particularly fond of that remarkable Amazonian parasite that a bloke told me about in the Volcano last week so it must be true. This parasite can swim up a stream of urine, take a grip, wriggle into the urethra and, well, you can imagine the rest, but I'd advise you not to.

Carcorp is lying. Spectacularly. Mr and Mrs Safari-Armpit buy Carcorp's cars because nature is nasty. Carcorp's cars shelter them from its brute indifference. Carcorp's cars ford rivers, scale scree, flatten saplings and pollute the world, while Mr and Mrs Safari-Armpit sit in air-conditioned comfort listening to Vivaldi.

None of this matters, of course. Carcorp's slogan is no worse than ads for toilet-tissue happiness or deodorant-driven sex, but it does seem to me to be a neat irony, that a company whose products are the brilliant inventions of scientific human reasoning should need to use emotional lies to sell them.

A betting man

When Jono Gibbes was a first year at secondary school he laid a bet. He bet a friend a thousand dollars that he would become an All Black.

When I was a first year at secondary school I, too, laid a bet. I bet Dave Collier a thousand pounds that we would never reach the senior year at school.

Mr Gibbes's bet was based on his ability at rugby. My bet was based on Hammersley. Hammersley was head prefect. As far as I knew he didn't have a Christian name. Nor did he need one. Hammersley was plenty.

I saw and heard him for the first time on stage in a school assembly. He had a voice like the fat string on a cello. He also had sideburns. From 20 yards away those sideburns looked like possums. From 10 yards away you could see them growing.

There were seven years between me and Hammersley, and a mountain range called puberty which I couldn't imagine ever crossing. Hammersley was a man.

By being a man Hammersley belonged to a group that included teachers. Teachers were less impressive than Hammersley. Their teeth were the colour of tobacco and so were their jackets. Those jackets had leather patches on the elbows. Some of the teachers had herbicidal halitosis. The rest had homicidal halitosis. And most of the teachers sagged. Hammersley didn't sag. He bristled. Nevertheless both teachers and Hammersley were men.

So were fathers. Some fathers bristled, others sagged, but most were just remote figures. My own had been born in the First World War and fought in the second. Not surprisingly, he never mentioned the former, but neither did he mention the latter. He seemed to have no past. He was, I think, a kind man and a good one, but to me he seemed distant, a member of that unthinkable adult tribe that I could not imagine joining.

In theory, of course, I knew that I had to become a man, but in practice I couldn't believe it. Men were a different species. When I looked at Hammersley or teachers or my father, I felt as caterpillars must feel when they see butterflies.

What made men so different was their apparent lack of emotions. Principal among these was fear. Men were never frightened. If something had threatened Hammersley, he would have merely sprouted another sideburn, sounded a bass note on the cello and sent the enemy scuttling.

We did see occasional frightened teachers. Dave Collier got under the skin of one man until he shook. When he wrote on the board the straight lines looked like the printout from a seismograph. He didn't last long. I hope they found him a nice bed. But the existence of such weaklings actually confirmed me in my belief that some males never made it to manhood.

The only emotion that proper men displayed was anger. Anger was rare, volcanic and dangerous, but you could see it coming. The mountain started to glow and pulse and spit gouts of lava, and then it was time for children to retreat.

Last weekend Jono Gibbes played for the All Blacks and finally won his bet. And thirty years ago I reached the last year at school and lost mine. Shortly afterwards an article appeared in the school magazine. I can quote one line of it exactly. It came from a collection of first impressions of new pupils at the school. 'And then we lined up for dinner,' wrote one eleven-year-old, 'and we were prodded by prefects and they were enormous, just like men.' He was writing about us, about Dave Collier and me.

I don't know if Jono Gibbes has received his thousand smackers, but I never paid Dave Collier his. This was partly because I didn't have the money, and partly because Dave forgot. But mainly because I've never felt that I actually lost. Though the first years saw us as men, I didn't. And I still don't. I am now well over twice the age of the sideburned Hammersley. My father's dead and I'm five years older than he was when I was born. I'm as bald as most of my teachers. But I'm still readily frightened. And I still feel like a child.

And the few schoolfriends I've kept in touch with still seem like children to me. Some sag, some bristle, all are battered, but they are still recognisable as the vulnerable, fear-prone, error-prone children they were.

Is all adulthood a sham, a theatrical role, a performance to daunt the tinies? Was Hammersley as vulnerable as I am? I suppose he was. But still it doesn't seem so. Still it seems that when my generation came of age the world of men shrank. A tribe of heroes and ogres passed from the earth and left behind a race of scuttling pygmies. It seemed so apt that the boy who became head prefect in my final year, the boy who tried to play the role that Hammersley had played, to fill the ten-league boots that Hammersley had worn, went by the name of Weatherseed. We knew him as Budgie.

Night-time angels

Do you have night-time angels? I do. Mine are good at crosswords.

I like a cryptic crossword but often there will be one clue that baffles me. I'll pursue a line of thinking that appears to be the right one but that brings me up against a wall of wrongness. So I will leave the clue alone a while and think of other things, then readdress it. But when I readdress it I will find my head pursuing the selfsame route for a second time, then a third time, a whole series of times, until it is sore from butting the unshiftable and I'll retire to bed bleeding with defeat and jeered every step of the way by the incomplete grid.

Then in the night the angels come. They take the chance to work when my stubbornness is sleeping. And in the morning as I shuffle to the source of coffee and fill a cup and idly spot the crossword, up pops the answer as fresh and surprising and clean as a morning mushroom. It's all the angels' work.

But they're not so good at careers. Last night a woman asked me what I'd like to be if I had all of human history to choose from. I could be pharaoh or pharisee, fisherman or fakir, anything I liked. I said I didn't know.

The night-time angels did. And now, on this dark winter morning when the cat is more than usually keen to leap onto the desk and type with its paws, the angels have pronounced. If I had all the choices in the history of human life I'd like to be a wandering minstrel. A troubadour.

I'd own nothing but a lute, a dog, a horse, a hat and a headful of songs. Illiterate, lice-racked. I would travel from pre-medieval village to pre-medieval village, climbing on arrival to some point of prominence, a balcony above the village square perhaps, or, on my naughtier days, a loaded gibbet. I'd strum a chord or two as an aesthetic bait to lure the stinking peasants, and then I'd sing the news. And what news. None of the pettiness of the mundane, but grand and sweeping news, made memorable by rhyme and tune and art. I'd sing of kings whose bodies rotted underneath their finery, of some ancient lover cutting off a finger and sending it by bird of paradise to her he loved. I'd sing of wars and famines, avalanches and the luminous ghosts of fish.

The peasants down below would gawp and coo and cackle as appropriate and toss me buns and pennies and would stroke my dog. On good days they would give me flagons full of ale and for the night a truckle bed of hay.

On bad days I would have to mount my horse and gallop out of town, my head held low behind the horse's neck to miss the hail of ribaldry and flung things. I'd seek a hedge to sleep beneath, all wet and shivering and wrapped around my dog.

Yes, that would be the life, a life of rapid ups and downs and rootlessness, with no diurnal work, but only risk and fear and sudden headspin joy.

But the angels are impractical. For starters I am terrified of horses. No herbivores have need of teeth as big as those. For another thing I am not brave. And for a third and final thing, I know I cannot sing.

I'd love to sing. I try to constantly. With beer inside me I can't resist the karaoke mike. But I murder every song.

I once took singing lessons. I yearned to play a luscious part in *Cabaret*, the part played in the film by Joel Gray, the part of the MC. So slinky, zestful, packed with acid, comic, perspicacious and a sexual omnivore – in short a catalogue of greatness.

I went to a woman who sings like a bubbling spring and I said teach me, and I flung dollars at her for a series of five lessons. But I attended only three. When I sang what she sang I could hear my notes were wrong but I was powerless to right them. She said the nicest things but she was lying. I ran at tunes just as I ran at crossword clues until my forehead bled from butting against the unshiftable bricks of inability.

I think I hoped that if I persevered the angels of the night might come and sweetly readjust the faulty tuning forks that occupy my head. I hoped in vain. The angels never came. They never will.

Why it is that we should yearn for what we cannot do and at the same time undervalue what we can, I cannot tell you. All I know is that if I could I would sing you a song. 'No wandering minstrel I,' I'd sing, 'no thing of rags and patches.' But I think I'll just start a crossword. The angels can finish it.

Hello, heat

Heat's back. Hello, heat. Laden with steam and indolence it swung down yesterday from the waistband of the globe, dumped its wet on the Alps then came to my house. It came like an oven-door openmg.

I drew the blinds. The heat laid siege, slowly. It seeped through the cracks and went everywhere and stayed. It occupied the middle and the corners. It filled the space under my desk, made my feet slide on my sandals. It turned the dog's water bowl on the deck to the temperature of blood. It killed insects and sprinkled the water with the corpses. They floated like tiny screws of paper, wispy, spent, burnt.

My dog has a black fur coat. In the heat she was like Trotsky in Mexico. Unlike Trotsky she couldn't shed her coat. The air heated her up, flopped her down, opened her jaws and tweaked out her tongue. The heat drove her under the house and pushed her over onto her side, panting.

Down below in the port it made windscreens into fireflashes. It made vinyl car seats screamingly untouchable. It made supermarket bags pudgy.

I am a cool climate man. I don't mind warmth. But warmth isn't heat. Warmth is a kindness. Warmth says do. Heat says don't.

Hot countries are poor countries. Samoa is poor. El Salvador's poor. Sudan is very poor. In hot countries they put on long white cotton shirts and sit down. They sit in the shade with a hat and a beer and patience. Sit it out. Try not to bother. Sit it out. Heat bleaches and saps. Bleaches the land, saps the will.

At twenty-one I went teaching in Spain and met heat for the first time. It was heat like brass. I didn't know what to do. I didn't know to do nothing. I flitted from shade patch to shade patch. I taught in the Spanish summer as I would in a Danish winter. I taught till the sweat darkened the crotch of my trousers, till my neck boiled with boils.

The fan in my classroom broke down one morning. I was teaching six middle-aged women. They conferred, then took pity. They took me away to an underground bar and fed me beer and a cold omelette. They taught me fretlessness. It doesn't matter, said the women. Today it is hot. That is all it is.

The only hot countries that are rich are the countries with oil. They were poor countries for ever, but then the busy greedy pale men came from the cool places with equipment made of metal that grew too hot to be handled. The pale men drilled through the rock and laid pipelines, sucking the liquefied heat of the desert away to put feeling in the fingers of the north. The locals took the money and sat in the shade of their thick white walls to drink sweet tea and watch the pale men being busy.

Last year I went to Singapore. The heat there was wet. The air wouldn't take my sweat. It was too full. It was always an inch away from rain, sudden, brief and rampant rain that was warm and that

126

drenched and then stopped. After it had stopped the island steamed. I hated all of it.

Yesterday I had to work. I worked badly, listless with heat. The keyboard was sticky. My head was torpid. Invention wilted. There was grit in the vees between my fingers. The desk fan skimmed ash from the ashtray. I gave up and drove the dog to the bay. The road ahead of us danced with black heat.

My dog ran into the water to shoulder depth then just stood there, reviving. One minute in water took a decade off her age. Cool again, she bounded through the wavelets like a spring-loaded puppy, like a lithe black dolphin.

Two women lay on their backs on towels, like starfish in bikinis, surrendering as if dead. Few men do that. I think some women are reptiles.

I swam with my dog. She snorts as she swims. I like to swim on my side to watch her legs working under water. Dogs don't really swim. Naturally buoyant, they just float and run. My old dog can swim for miles.

The soil of the path behind the bay was dried to talcum powder. The leaves of the sheltering trees, still pale green and spring tender, diffused the sunlight to something gentle. But you could sense the effect of the sun on them. You could sense them darkening, thickening, ageing. Two months from now they'll be leathery. Four months and they'll crackle underfoot.

Back home and the house was a vat of heat. I fed myself, fed my dog, then stripped and lay on my bed, sweating, riding it out.

Probe and rectify, please

When Prue from the Therapeutic Massage Association rang to ask if I would like a therapeutic massage, I thought that I wouldn't. But I also thought of baboons.

I've always envied baboons. Not for the purple buttocks, though there are occasions when a couple of those could prove handy, or at least entertaining, but for the way baboons groom each other. They pass hot African afternoons poring over each other's flesh, running their prehensile fingers through the fur, extracting ticks and eating them.

I'm not frantic to eat ticks but I would like to be at ease with touch. Touch is potent. If I am working at my desk and someone unexpectedly lays hands on my shoulders, a spasm of distaste makes my muscles cringe and tense. And I can still remember from adolescence a hand placed casually on my forearm that stood the hairs on my neck to attention and triggered a month of lovesick sleeplessness.

So when Prue offered me a therapeutic massage, I dithered.

'But,' said Prue, 'you'll enjoy it and it will make you feel good and it will cost you nothing.' So I said yes.

Frances operates from what looks like a garage. She has a diploma in therapeutic massage. Whether this makes her a masseur or a masseuse or just someone with a diploma in therapeutic massage, I didn't ask. I just called her Frances. She was infectiously cheerful.

The garage had anatomical posters on the wall, carpet on the floor and a table on the carpet. The air was warm and awash with subliminal new-age musak that I didn't like but soon stopped noticing.

I completed a have-you-ever-suffered-from-any-of-these form that made me wonder how I'd survived so long, wrote no for everything, stripped to my underpants and lay on my front on the table. Frances draped me with towels. My face rested in a padded basketball hoop.

Then Frances warmed her hands, smeared them with almond oil, shifted a towel in the manner of a morgue attendant seeking identification and set to work on a leg. Her thumbs ploughed through my muscles like the prow of a ship through a sea of soft rubber.

When I asked her why she used almond oil she said it was just personal taste. 'Some people use apricot oil,' she said, 'or grapeseed oil.'

I said I used grapeseed oil to fry sausages.

'So do I,' she said.

In my right calf she found what I sensed to be a medium density lump. When she pressed it, it felt a bit sore.

'That feels a bit sore,' I said.

'I know,' she said.

Then she asked me whether I wanted a superficial feel-good

massage or a deep one that would probe and rectify the sore and lumpy bits.

'Probe and rectify,' I said.

'You'll feel it in the morning,' she said and her thumbs plunged. It felt as though she were parting sheaves of muscle fibre in order to get at the undersheaves. She returned to the knotted lumpy bit and leant on it till it burned with a low-intensity doing-me-good pain. Gradually the lump dissolved, as if melting under heat and pressure.

When she'd finished with the leg she asked if it felt lighter. By now I was as keen as a dog to please. I waved the leg around a bit.

'I don't know,' I said.

After she'd rootled around on the other leg for a minute or two I told her that she had found a sore spot somewhere but that I wasn't going to tell her where it was.

'Let's see if my thumbs return to it,' she said, which sounded altogether too mystical for me. Her thumbs returned to it.

She compressed my buttocks agreeably for a bit then moved up my back. When she reached the shoulder I told her of an ancient injury that still niggles. She replied with an anatomical analysis that sounded reassuringly medical and followed it up with some lovely lump-melting stuff in the area that Mr Spock uses to kill people.

I rolled over and she did the front of my legs and then asked if I'd like my stomach done. I said yes. She told me she'd attended a three-day course on stomach massage. When I asked what there was in stomach muscles to occupy three days, she explained how it was possible to rummage under the muscles to get at the internal organs. Shortly afterwards she told me my stomach was very tense.

When she'd done with me she asked how long I thought I'd been on the table. I said about an hour. It had been almost two.

130

'So how do you feel?' she asked.

I said I wasn't sure and I thanked her and I left.

A little way along the road I stopped my car and went walkabout. I wanted to feel how I felt. I felt loose. I felt light on my feet. And I felt about half an inch taller.

I slept like a baby, one of those babies that smell faintly of almonds. In the morning I felt dandy. I took the dogs up the hill as I do every day. I loped up that hill like a baboon.

McFilm

I knew there was something wrong with film as a medium and Hollywood as culture when I was taken to see *101 Dalmatians* at the age of eight. Twenty minutes into the film I erupted screaming from my seat, ran home, grabbed the family dog, barricaded myself under the bed and refused to emerge until puberty. Apart, that is, from nipping out at the age of eleven to see *Where Eagles Dare* twice. I went the second time only to confirm that it was as bad as it had seemed the first time. It was.

Offhand I can think of only three films I've seen that I would happily see again: *Cabaret*, *My Life as a Dog* (which has little to do with dogs) and *If*.

If tells the story of a revolution at a crusty boarding school. I once tried to rent *If* when I was teaching in a similarly crusty boarding school in Canada. Most of the little darlings I was teaching were merely shoppers in embryo, salivating at the prospect of acquiring the latest hugely advertised gewgaw that the industrial complex had cooked up to shrivel their tiny minds. I thought *If* might shake one or two of them at the roots of their consumerist complacency.

Fat chance twice over. First, a fat chance of undoing a dozen years of televisual brainwashing. Even back then, Canada had the biggest shopping mall in the world, and liked to boast about it. It was somewhere in Alberta. Maybe it *was* Alberta. And second, a fat chance of actually finding a copy of *If*.

At the local video store I was offered 3000 indistinguishable Hollywood megabusters starring good old Sly or Arnie acting the Neanderthal with hi-tech weaponry and a death-per-minute rating to eclipse the Battle of the Somme.

But that's film for you. Film does shallow emotive nonsense splendidly. What it doesn't do is serious thoughtful sense.

Most film is ephemeral, superficial pap, a sort of visual Prozac. It's eye-candy, bereft of substance. The reason for this poverty is that film struggles to render complex interior humanity. That's the domain of literary fiction. But literary fiction doesn't stand a hope against film. It asks too much work of the reader. The future is six-gun Arnie and you're welcome to him. If you want me I'll be up the hill in a cave reading Jonathan Franzen.

Of course some films do try to do the stuff that literature does. Most of them fail. You get twee versions of Jane Austen with lawns and horses and muslin dresses with the waistline just below the bust so the women all look like shuttlecocks. What you don't get is waspish old Jane sticking the knife into her gargoyle creations.

Or else you get dark and moody art house cinema filmed on the fjord-ravaged coast of Norway where women with blow-drier hair stand on cliff tops and look longingly at seagulls. And as you crane to read the semi-literate subtitles you are surrounded by such awful film buffs braying about symbolism in their polo-neck sweaters that you half hope for Arnie to wander in, grunt and mow them down while oiling his biceps.

And then there's the fantasy. Cinema has always done fantasy. There's the romantic fantasy stuff to gratify the yearning breasts of disappointed women, stuff in which Cary Grant, or his brother Hugh, arrives with immaculate grooming to lay the heroine tenderly amid the cool sheets of paradise. Then there's the adventure fantasy in which Indiana Tarzan does unlikely things to bad people who want to do unspeakable things to him. And increasingly there's the altogether elsewhere fantasy like *Lord of the Rings*. Harmless stuff in its way, a sort of Wombles with blood, but hardly a pinnacle of cultural achievement. Not that that bothers the devotees who are flocking to New Zealand with their little knapsacks and their locations guide and their cheese and pickle sandwiches to make reverential pilgrimages to the spot of turf out the back of Ashburton where Dopo drew his enchanted sword and slew the mighty Torpor, leader of the Woks.

Nor does it bother the government. There's money in those knapsacks. And so our leaders are now offering tax breaks to Hollywood. As a result it seems likely that New Zealand will stop being Middle Earth and will become the set for *The Lion, the Witch and the Infantile Regression Syndrome*, and who knows what other barren little entertainments to take our minds off an overpopulated planet.

I never did find *If*. After traipsing round Video Hut and McVideo and Kentucky Fried Video and finding nothing but multiple copies of the same mindless guff, I went home and used the phone. The first three stores I rang had never heard of *If*. The girl in the fourth store asked me to repeat the title. And then she asked me to spell it.

My last hope was an outfit called Red Hot Videos. 'Have you,'

I asked down the phone, 'by any chance, got a copy of a film made in the sixties called *If*?'

'Hold on,' said the man. He returned a minute later. 'Sorry, no,' he said, 'but we have got one called *F*. Will that do?'

Arachnametaphor

The spider had spun a web across my wing-mirror. Presumably it hoped to catch female flies.

I admire spiders. I admire the way they bungy gently from ceiling to floor. And I admire even more the way they reverse bungy to the ceiling by eating the rope. I admire the way they torture flies. (I am soft on animals but flies don't count. I like the thought of a fly becoming soup while retaining consciousness.) I admire the static trawlers that are spider webs. And I particularly admire the way non-venomous spiders inspire terror in human beings 3 billion times their size.

I taught a child who went on to become an All Black. If there was a spider in the classroom this child left the classroom. He left it at a speed that later served him well. He scattered desks like would-be tacklers. His exits were so memorable it was worth importing spiders specially.

I am not an arachnophobe. But neither am I an arachnophile. I share with most of the population, it seems, an arachnoslightuneasiness. Small spiders do not trouble me. Indeed they are welcome in my house because of our shared enmity to flies. If I spot a spider the size of a ten-cent piece on my bedroom ceiling, I blow it a kiss, wish it sweet dreams, turn off the light and sleep the deep sleep of a man without worries. But if the spider is the size of a fifty-cent piece and possessed of legs that arch like the McDonald's logo, then I will rise from my virgin bachelor sheets and capture the thing in a glass and transport it to the garden at arm's length with a slightly wrinkled nose – my own, that is, not the spider's, whose nose I never remember to study – and I will toss it well away from me and scamper back and shut the door behind me and hope the spider doesn't know how to work the cat flap.

The spider on the wing mirror was a twenty-cent piece spider. As I reversed down the drive its value shrank. By the time I was on the open road and heading for the beach with the dogs in the back and a song on my lips, the spider had suffered serious inflation. Diameterwise it was worth less than five cents. It had appraised the situation and gathered itself into a ball.

Though actually I doubt that it did much appraising. The events were beyond a spider's appraising scope. The beast had gone to bed on the wing mirror confident that it had found somewhere solid to hang up its hat for a while. Then it awoke to find that somewhere bowling along the open road. It was as if I had awoken to find the whole of Lyttelton jogging to Sydney. And if that were to occur I expect that, like the spicler, I would curl into a ball and whimper. Not of course that I could tell whether the spider was whimpering. The window between us acted as a barrier to sound. And it was too cool a morning to wind it down to study the audible grief of a spider.

Rolling into a ball as a form of defence is a common tactic and a good one. Spiders, woodlice and people being kicked do it. Hedgehogs do it particularly well, whether they're being kicked or, as is now cornmon in these parts, being hunted by my new dingbat of a dog. But it takes a lot to dissuade a dingbat. The dog picks up the coiled hedgehog, brings it to me in triumph and looks up at me with eyes beseeching praise, tail going like a flag in a gale and tongue gently dripping blood. When I lean down to congratulate the dog on his devoted stupidity, I sometimes hear the tightly curled hedgehog giggling.

I am confident the wing-mirror spider wasn't giggling. It was too busy clinging with eight legs. Aerodynamically a sphere is a better shape than a spider's usual posture, but it still can't be a doddle to retain a grip at 80 kilometres an hour when your usual top speed is 80 metres a day. But though its web went west, the spider hung on.

The dogs and I frolicked on the beach for an hour. When we came back the spicler was still on the mirror. I drove home gently, believing the spider had been through enough for one day.

All that was yesterday. This morning when I went out with the dog to fetch the newspaper, I noted that the spider was still on the wing mirror. Indeed it had recovered sufficiently from its trauma to spin itself another web, and all without so much as a single counselling session.

So what? Well, I am tempted to see the spider as a metaphor. For what? For everything. Go about your business, it suggests. You will make monumental errors, like setting up house on a swift-moving mirror, but don't let the fear of error dissuade you. When things go wrong, as they will, hang on tight. The storm will pass. And when it's passed, just start again. That's all.

But I shall resist the temptation of metaphor. Partly because it's only a spider. But mainly because on my way back up the drive with the paper, I killed it.

Dinnerhoea

Fourteen years ago I was twice his age but now I'm not. I still don't understand how that could be, which was why I taught him English instead of Maths.

When I say I taught him English, I wouldn't want you to imagine that I taught him any, well, English. By the time I got to stand in front of the little brute, he was sixteen years old and already spoke and wrote the language. It was like being plonked in front of Einstein and being told you had a year to train him to use a calculator. All that was required of me was a bit of show-offery like spelling diarrhoea.

I like diarrhoea. The word has a grisly onomatopoeic beauty. I also like onomatopoeic. And I despise the way Americans take the 'o' out of diarrhoea, thereby destroying the diphthong. I like the word diphthong, too, though I bet the Yanks take the first 'h' out of it, thereby turning the language from a rich thick beer into a Miller's Bloody Lite.

And as for the Simplified Spelling nutters who want to make English into some sort of safe phonetic shopping mall, well, I wish them nothing less than a bowt of diareya so spektakyular and protrakted that thay grone til there dipfongs ake. Then perhaps they might understand that the majestic complexity of English spelling is nothing more nor less than a hurdles race in which the first hurdle is set at dog and the last at diarrhoea, and the hurdle at which any competitor falls is as sure a guide to their moral worth as I know.

And don't give me any nonsense about dyslexia. The English language is a hard master, not given to handkerchiefs, hugs or counselling, as evidenced by the delicious difficulty of spelling dyslexia, not to mention the 's' in lisp, though I now find that I have mentioned it. Nor do I want to hear any bleating about spellchecks. I've just run the spellcheck over this. It highlightecl 'spellcheck' because the greedy little programme wanted to turn itself into two words, which it doesn't deserve and isn't going to get so long as I'm in charge, and it also highlighted the jokes. Spellchecks don't get jokes. Their little binary chips get as flustered as Bill Gates confronted by a piece of poetry.

Anyway the half-my-age lad, who is now neither of those things, wants to go out to dinner. Tonight. It was his idea. He sent me an email out of that famously unpredictable colour, the blue. Let's do dinner, he said, which is the sort of English I like a lot.

He was a clever child. He was also funny. Of course, I wasn't having any of that being funny stuff in my classroom, where it was my job to be funny and his job to laugh and to learn how to spell diarrhoea.

But he was funny in his essays. Very few children are funny in their essays, or at least very few are funny when they try to be. He even wrote funny stuff about Shakespeare. Shakespeare would have liked funny stuff about Shakespeare more than he would have liked earnest stuff about Shakespeare.

Anyway this lad is still writing funny essays and they are being published and now he wants to go for dinner. I am looking forward to it, which is absurd because I know exactly how it will be. We will meet in the bar and we will shake hands and he will think but not say how bald I have grown (though grown seems the opposite of the correct verb) and my side of the conversation will run like this:

Hello . . . Oh, thank you. A beer . . . No, anything but a Miller's Lite, actually . . . Cheers. So, er well, tell me, what have you been, sort of, you know, up to, since I last, well, saw you? . . . I see . . . Oh really. Did you like Peru? . . . I see. Ha ha . . . Oh, really. And did you like Cambodia? . . . I see, really. Would you care for another? . . . Right, where were we? Hindustan, wasn't it? . . . Oh, that's right, Glasgow . . . Oh really, did she? Gosh . . . And what happened to the goat? . . . What, me? Nothing to tell really. One of my dogs died. That's about it, I think . . . No, I don't. Twenty years teaching is more than enough for anyone . . . No, I don't remember him . . . No, I don't remember him . . . No, I don't remember him . . . Well, actually I was a bit afraid of you, too . . . No, really, I was . . . Nice of you to say that, but it isn't true . . . No, I mean it, I didn't teach you a thing . . . Okay, tell me one thing I actually taught you . . . Brilliant. I'd forgotten about that. Did you know the Yanks leave the 'o' out? . . . Oh, did I? Let's have a lot more drinks.

Ridiculously excited

I have bought a new television. It is the third television of my life and I am waiting for it to arrive now. I am ridiculously excited.

When I bought my first television I was also ridiculously excited. That television was old and cheap and the size of a small horse. I was excited by its bigness. But when I got it home its bigness embarrassed me. I tried to disguise that bigness by putting a pot plant on it. I hoped people would say, 'What a nice pot plant.' They didn't. They said, 'What a big television. Oh, and your pot plant's dying.'

Watering a plant is not gratifying. When you feed a dog it wags its tail. When you buy a man a drink he wags his tail too. But when you water a plant it does nothing. So I generally forget to. And when I do remember, I tend to drown the thing.

I have watched many plants die and it is not a spectacular process. But I have watched only one television die, my horse-sized one. Its death wasn't a process but it was spectacular. It happened when I watered the plant. The bang made the cat disappear for a week. When the smoke cleared the plant seemed fine.

My second television was brand-new, with a remote control. I was ridiculously excited by it. And because my first telly was embarrassingly big I replaced it with a dwarf one. I hoped people would say, 'My word, what a tiny television. You must be a terribly cerebral person with no time for the lurid gewgaws of contemporary trash culture.' They didn't. They said, 'Why don't you get a decent-sized television?'

Then last year my tiny telly shrank. I found that during a rugby match I could no longer read the score in the corner of the screen. Of course that's not a problem when England are playing because you know they will be winning, but for other games it's annoying.

Then last week a woman visited me. She picked up my remote control. 'This is filthy,' she said. I chose not to argue.

The woman went to the kitchen and fetched one of those squirty things that turns cheap detergent into excitingly expensive detergent. She squirted the remote control a few times and rubbed it till it gleamed like an ornament. Which was fortunate because the remote control had become an ornament.

Once you've had a remote control it's tedious not to have one. It's like having your dog go deaf.

So I went shopping and I struck it lucky. I wasn't served by any ordinary sales person. I was served by a sales consultant. He was about nineteen and he had what may have been Marmite on his shirt.

I askecl him why one of the televisions was a lot cheaper than the others. He said it didn't have a wide screen or a flat screen. Apparently a wide screen lets you see what's going on at the edges of movies and a flat screen lets you watch from an oblique angle. I said I was an old-fashioned type. I liked the stuff in the middle of movies and I tended to sit square on to the screen. 'Then that's the telly for you,' he said. You can see why he became a consultant so young.

I shop in the same way as I water plants. I don't do it often but when I do I tend to do lots of it quickly. This is partly because once I have forced myself into a shop I feel like a terrier in a barrel of rats. But it is also because I imagine that if I do a lot of shopping now, I won't have to do any more for a long time. So along with a television I bought a video player and a wall bracket to support them both.

I asked if the wall bracket was easy to assemble. The consultant said it was a piece of cake.

Pieces of cake don't normally come with instructions. Nor did the wall bracket. Instead it came with a list of the 7000 bits that were in the box. The list was helpfully translated into six languages. I was pleased to learn that the German for domed shakeproof nut is gesicherte hutmutter. It sounds like a dried scoutmistress.

But there was also a set of easy-to-follow diagrams which enabled me to assemble the thing and fix it rigidly to the wall before you could say two broken drill bits, quite a lot of blood and the whole of one Sunday.

But now I'm sitting with my scoutmistresses unshakeably fixed and I am looking out for the television delivery man with a sense of ridiculous excitement. I particularly look forward to discovering what new form of disappointment awaits me.

Necks, please

I've got an inexplicable bad neck. Went to sleep last night with a neck so pliant I had ostriches asking me my secret, but awoke this Sunday morning with a neck like a crankshaft – not that I quite know what a crankshaft is, but if it's as inflexible and knobbly as I imagine it to be, then it's bang right. Perhaps I should ring an osteopath – not that I quite know what an osteopath is either.

And anyway I expect osteopaths play golf on Sunday, swinging their spine-straight clubs with such smug rubberiness that they drum up custom even on the Sabbath – not that I'm quite sure what the Sabbath is, since Jews, I believe, think it's Saturday, Gentiles Sunday, and teenagers the name of a rock group. I could look it up, I suppose, along with crankshaft and osteopath, but the dictionary's down there to my right and I'm up here at my desk nursing my neck, and the fear of pain beats the thirst for knowledge. Injury does that. The world shrinks to the point of pain and nothing else matters.

By swivelling my eyes, which is the only form of exercise I feel up to, I can see birds with irritatingly good necks. Greenfinches are clinging to the seed bell I thoughtfully hang for them, and jabbing at it with necks all lissome and enviable. They keep their balance by fluttering one wing. I didn't realise birds could move their wings independently, although if you think about it, which I'm doing for the first time, it makes sense. I mean, if you wave your right arm, the left one doesn't flap in sympathy. It would make carpentry tricky.

Anyway I can't remember ever seeing a bird with a crook neck, though I've seen plenty with crooked necks, most notable among which are shags, herons and bitterns. Shags fold their necks into an 'S' when roosting, but straighten them in flight. Herons do the opposite. Bitterns, meanwhile, whose necks are habitually as crooked as snakes, stick them vertically into the air whenever they sense danger. The idea, apparently, is that they then resemble reeds. At which point the prowling predator says, 'Well, bugger me. Could have sworn there was a bittern round here but no, nothing but reeds. Guess I'll just go off to the beach and get myself a shag.'

Bitterns are rare birds and, to be frank, I'm not surprised. The reed-imitation gambit doesn't seem like a winner to me. Though I suppose it is just possible that bitterns are actually the most abundant birds in the world and what you and I imagine to be reed beds are in fact enormous flocks of bitterns. In which case, I suppose, bitterns may have been used over the years to thatch cottages, which is a picturesque notion so long as the bitterns didn't suddenly and collectively decide to migrate – not that I actually know whether bitterns migrate. I could look it up, of course, but the bird book's next to the dictionary.

Anyway I wouldn't make a very good bittern this morning. While mooching through the reed bed in search of a frog to spear for Sunday lunch, I'd sense the presence of a predator, a polecat, say – not that I'm quite sure what a polecat is – and I'd switch into reed mode. The polecat would catch the creaking of vertebrae, spot the reed with a wince on its face and a suspiciously feathered stem, and suddenly, well, once bitten no bittern, and one less bit of thatching for your cottage. Which perhaps explains why I've never seen any sort of bird with a crook neck. Though a bloke I met yesterday told me he once saw a duck pretending to be crippled. It was limping around begging bread from sympathetic children. But when the bread ran out, it straightened up and walked off a well duck. Good on it, I say, in this dog eat dog world, not, as it happens, that I've ever seen a dog eat a dog.

But I have seen chickens eat chicken. I used sometimes to collect a bucket of leftovers from the Volcano and bring it back for my chooks. They'd dive into the swill with gusto, flinging fish and peas and anchovies over their shoulders as they frantically rummaged for any morsel of their own kind. Not liking to think I had a backyard of clucking cannibals, I've stopped bringing them leftovers, but I've since discovered that chooks aren't choosy carnivores.

Only this week my dog threw up after chewing her morning cow bone. Dogs are supposed to return to their own vomit but Jessie never got a chance. Before you could say nausea, the gutsiest of my chooks had strutted up and was picking through . . . well, you don't need the details.

Which reminds me that I haven't got any food in the fridge which means that I'm going to have to go to the shops which means that I'm going to have to reverse out of the drive. And since my chances of twisting my neck to look over my shoulder when reversing are about as high as a bittern's chances of being mistaken for a reed, perhaps I should just sit in my front garden looking woebegone and hope that some sympathetic children pass by on their way to the duck pond, not that we've actually got a duck pond round here. Or many sympathetic children. It's all, to be frank, a pain in the neck.

Stuff love

Love and trust, you can keep them. Particularly love. I've had it with love.

There you are washed up on the blank beach of middle age like an empty Fanta bottle, discarded, turning brittle in the sun, ignored by the cackle-throated gulls, essentially an ex-thing, a husk, a was, when in sweeps the spring tide of love and lifts you off the beach and, whoa, suddenly you're flinging about like a teenage Fanta bottle, full of fizz and zest and cruel delusion. Well, stuff that. I'm not falling for it again. I'm going to buy myself an anchor and cling limpet-like to the beach for ever until, well, until the next spring tide rolls in and the whole caboodle runs its ghastly little up and down course again.

And as for trust, well, I'll get to that in a minute.

Love? Ha. And that's a ha with a curled lip and an ironic tone that it's tricky to convey on paper. You should see how hard I'm hitting the keys. Fair whacking them, I am. Like that. And that.

I didn't love the Subaru. Oh no. We were just friends. Familiar. Comfortable. Easy. 'Oh hello,' I'd say each morning, 'you still here? Good.' And off we'd putter to the grog shop for a drop of breakfast and everything was dandy. Nothing to upset the dreary round of routine; time passing as time does. Then suddenly, folly. Sheer lunatic folly. I fell for, well, I can't bring myself to type the name. Let's just say a car, a particular car. My tired flesh surged and pulsed with want. Primal stuff. Want want want. Want that retractable roof. Want that remote control key fob. Want those cupholders, that plethora of compartments for keeping things in, those fog lamps, those, God help me, bull bars.

Bull bars? Ha, again. I know I'm saying ha a lot, but that's because ha's exactly right. If these bull bars met a bull, they'd shrivel and crumple before you could say pretentious simulacrum of bogus masculinity. They're lamb bars, weasel bars, supermarket-shopping-trolley bars.

But I bought them. Oh yes, I shelled out the money that I love, to run my vein-mapped hands over them, to fondle their chromium curves. I was deaf, dumb, blind, stupid with love. Love is wilful. Love is obtuse. Love whisks you out of the top set – 'gifted' is what they call the clever ones, these days, gifted, ha – and dumps you in the intensive care remedial class alongside the boneheads and the thumb-suckers. And yet, you just don't care.

I gave the Subaru away. For zilch. For a beer. Three hundred thousand kilometres it had trundled with me in its belly and nary a whimper. It was merely and honourably functional, dependable, a Dobbin of the road, a plodder, and I gave it away like an empty Fanta bottle to Dave. Dave who's just passed his driving test. 'Here you are, son,' I said, '1800cc of turbocharged reliable freedom,' and he said ta and took it straight to the carwash as I never once did, never once, and then he parked it where I can see it from my window now, gleaming and sneering, my ex.

And in its stead, in place of old dependable, I've got this gadget-laden . . . thing. I'm exactly like that nonagenarian tetrazillionaire from Kansas who, when only a stumble short of the eternal land-fill, married a twenty-year-old strippeuse with implants.

Well, the old fool's dead now and so is love, my love. Or rather not dead, but transmuted into a smouldering hatred, rich as a diesel exhaust. I've only got to catch sight of those lamb bars, that high-mounted brake light, I've only got to hear the pre-pubertal beep beep beep the thing emits when it goes backwards, to seethe with loathing, disgust, disgust at self. Because that's what this car represents, of course, an abject lapse of self-awareness. 'This above all,' said whoever it was in Shakespeare, 'to thine own self be true, and it must follow, as the night the day, thou canst not then be false to any man.' Easy to say, and even easier to ignore.

So, yesterday I decided to lance the boil of love gone sour. I went to trade the thing in after less than a month. Round the ghastly car-yards of Moorhouse Avenue I went, which is exactly like snorkelling with sharks. But now I knew what I was looking for. My only criterion was that I mustn't love the thing. If my heart gave a little lurch at the sight of a car, I just walked on by. And I found what I wanted, a car so dull it's effectively invisible, a car so utilitarian and square that it looks more like a box than a box does.

The deal should happen tomorrow, if, that is, I can trust the dealer. Which reminds me, I said I'd anatomise trust. Well, that's a doddle. Trust? Same as love. Ha.

Where do you go to?

Sleep's good, especially at Christmas, but going to sleep is better. I know nothing more delicious than sliding from wake into sleep. It's a letting go, a submission. You let slip the constructed self, the armour that you don you each day to fight the world. As you fall asleep it slithers off as softly as a dress of silk. Even the hardest gang-man, the most shaven-headed, sex-tongued, greed-driven, hate-brimming, finger-jabbing, gun-stroking bully boy slides into softness each night, vulnerable as his own fraught psyche.

It's the journey into utter privacy, the time of most alone, like a hermit withdrawing deep into the darkness of the cave. And in the darkness up swims sleep. It's the oldest daily miracle.

How does it happen? How does the thug go to sleep? How do you? Do you count sheep? I doubt it. I have never met anyone who counts sheep. The conscious act of counting defies the rise of the mind that dreams.

I play cricket. Or rather every night I replay a little bit of cricket, a single moment that happened twenty years ago. I know exactly where the game was played. I can see the ground, the hedges that surround it, the long grass inside them, then the close-cut turf of the outfield half bleached by the summer, the fresher green of the square, the mower's stripes, the pitch itself. Lying in bed, I can feel the sun of twenty summers ago on my forearms.

I am batting. A young man runs in to bowl. His shirt is flapping. He leaps at the crease and bowls. The ball is overpitched, a half-volley, juicy as a summer plum. The air is spangle-bright. I can see the gold lettering on the ball, the raised stitches of the seam. I lean forward, drawn to the ball with a sort of midsummer ease. My movement has the pace of flowing honey. Like honey it is sweet and simple. Body and bat are one.

The sound of the ball in the bat's heart is as rich as a church bell. No jarring. No sense of impact. It is like a caress, a channelling of affection, and the ball's direction simply reverses. The ball has come to me and then it has gone away from me as I have desired that it should. I haven't hit the ball, I have expressed it. It feels as natural and as languid as a dog's stretch, as a river's flow.

At a speed that surprises me the ball scuds across the turf as straight as the hand of a clock. Mid-off makes a hopeless dive at it. His floundering clumsiness occupies a different realm to the progress of the ball from my bat to the field's far edge.

I take a stride or two up the pitch, knowing I've no need to run but doing so for form's sake. The ball's speed, its impetus, is mine. I am attached to it as it travels. It owes its movement to me. Look, I did that.

Forty, fifty, sixty yards away now, and it is still running on the fuel I fed it through the simple arc and flow of my body and my bat. It crosses the boundary and plunges into the long and withered grass of summer, where it comes to rest, held by a mesh of tangled stems that binds it like a cradle. It's made a nest, like a small animal.

I sent it there. And in my mind I join it there, in its nest of long grasses.

Its arrival upsets a tiny metropolis. It's the meteor that flattens New York. Ants, spiders, grasshoppers, a thousand insects I can't name, scurry for safety in the mulch of spent vegetation, frantic for the darkness and the rich moist soil. The ball waits. In my head I wait with it, waiting for the disturbance to subside in this miniature jungle.

Slowly peace returns. The spindly spider resumes its high-stepping progress through the stems, its arched legs as frail as its own gossamer. Ants go back to their co-operative business. Mites, woodlice and a million microscopic creatures re-emerge to scout and fossick through their tiny world. And I am among them, not moving, just seeing and being there, where no one cares or matters, where death is common and ordinary and regenerative and where no cricket scores ever penetrate, where no words are written, where no words exist, but where the endless web of brief and interdependent lives goes on going on. I sink into it. And as I sink the other self rises, the night-time self that can go anywhere with its strange alternative logic. I am asleep. Happy Christmas.

Balloooooooon

I flew to Rotorua to speak at a breakfast function. I arrived the afternoon before. My hosts met me at the airport and said come this way. I thought I would get drinks. I got Christmas decorations. We had to titivate the breakfast room. I was put in charge of blowing up balloons.

It must be ten years since I blew and tied a balloon, and thirty since I did so with any frequency. But like knotting a tie or skiing it proved to be a skill you never lose. As I gripped the little rubber nozzle between finger and thumb and sealed my lips around the little rubber rim, I was flung back through time as if down one of those corny swirling tunnels in a bad science fiction film. Everything was familiar, from the taste and smell and texture of the rubber, to the sense of imminent gaiety.

The only hard breath is the first breath. Sausage balloons in particular can be obstinate, remaining the size of peapods while your cheeks turn the colour of bruises and your eyeballs bulge. But these were round balloons. and round balloons are easy.

The balloon stiffens, momentarily resists, then suddenly, gratifyingly swells before your nose like an out-of-focus vegetable. And with it comes a noise, a sort of one-way roar like a distant engine. That noise says fun to come.

As the rubber stretches, its colour thins from rich to pale, from ruby to pink, from National Party blue to thin spring sky.

You pinch the nozzle to trap the air and you hold the half-inflated balloon in front of you. It's a breast, rounded by the laws of physics and tipped with a nipple, a protuberance of still-dense colour. The flesh yields easily to the touch, moulding, not taut.

A few more breaths and the breast is a pregnancy, hugely swollen, tautly burstable, belly-buttoned and exciting. As the thing grows to block your vision it is tempting to bail out early. You must not bail out early. You must blow that critical extra breath, the one that makes the pregnancy grow a stem, turning a sphere into a pear. It's the peak of inflation and like all peaks it's the moment of greatest danger. You have to judge the exact point between not enough and too much. Not enough and the thing is never a true balloon. It is too small, too dense, a fraction too heavy. Too much and suddenly there's no balloon, only shocked nerves and laughter and a scattering of damp rubber. It's the thrilling razor-edge of harmless peril.

Get it right, get the pear when it's ripe, and a balloon's a rich fat thing. You take it from your mouth and grip it lightly between your thighs. It squeaks like a shoe-sole on linoleum. As you loop the nozzle round and through itself to seal it, sometimes it slips from the fingers and, hey presto, a flying fart. The fart does momentary random loop-the-loops, belching hilarity, and then it's down, floored, scuppered, limp and silent.

You laugh and pick it up again. It's warm. You reinflate it, more easily now that the rubber is stretched and dimpled. You clutch it a tad more tightly between the thighs, tie the knot, pull it tight and then just let it go. What you've made is a wonder. It almost floats. It doesn't fall. It drifts. It's captive happiness. It's impossible to resist batting it.

When you bat it it goes ping, a unique noise, a noise of childhood. It goes away when batted, but slowly and not far. It wants to play.

It begs for a game. It stirs the infant self.

Gravity has hauled at your flesh for years, has slowed you down, withered and bent you, made you ugly. But gravity only grazes a balloon. It's crockery you can drop without consequences. It's a world made soft and pointless, a cartoon world.

A balloon's an equaliser. Everyone's a superstar soccer player, one who can keep the ball aloft with head and shoulder and chest and heel for minutes on end. The cruel rules are in suspension. You're close to the weightless moon of playtime.

Be gentle, says the balloon, wait, I shall come down. And if, as it sinks in its own good gentle time, you swing a real-time toot with real-time venom and volley the balloon with all your muscle-swung might, it scoffs. It goes perhaps a yard at speed, then slows and drifts again, ridiculously soon. It's held and fragile, as temporary as happiness and as good.

Balloons either burst or seep. The held air scatters or leaks. Balloons aren't built to last. They aren't possessable. They exist in the present tense, for fun now, while you can.

The organisers of the breakfast were all as old as I or older, with warts and worries and doctors' appointments. But as the balloons were blown and tied we waded through them laughing at their rulelessness and playing pointless games and being children, now.

The breakfast was okay. But the balloons were better.

Glossy lala

I don't know whether it was an advertising stunt or an accident or a threat but someone left a pornographic magazine in my letterbox. It's as glossy as a yacht and the weight of a paving slab. Rolled up it could be issued to the riot squad. But it's what's inside that's so devastating.

I am not easily shocked but I was shocked. I can only give thanks that I got to it before the local kiddiwinks did. If freedom of speech dictates that such stuff must be published it should at least be sold under brown paper covers and only to adults with a certificate signed by three psychologists testifying to the purchaser's imperturbable mental stability. The magazine in question is the Christmas issue of *House and Garden*.

The cover features a festive board – yes, that's the sort of language we're dealing with here – groaning – of course – under bowls of soup with swirls of cream in them, glasses of fresh-poured bubbly, lit green candles in a decorative candelabrum beneath a decorative chandelier and beside a decorative centrepiece of Christmas lilies and I don't know what else because I had to avert my eyes. In the background are chairs festooned with cushions,

cushions so winsome that I felt the catch in the throat that warns of trouble to come.

I should never have read the text on the cover. I read the text on the cover. Here it is in full: 'Gorgeous table tops. Deck your halls (I am not making this up). Angels and tiaras. (No, really, I am not making this up.) Perfect puddings. Wrap it in an heirloom.'

And inside, well it was everything you could expect and worse. And where do I begin? I shall begin with the prurient glimpses into other people's houses. Either this stuff is all fictional, the people and the places they live in entirely knocked up for the purposes of selling magazines, or else there are two varieties of human beings, two varieties that have diverged so radically by the process of evolution that they can barely recognise each other, and I belong to the other variety. Here is a world where beds are made, pillows creaseless and 'in Wendy's wardrobe European shoes are lined up with military precision'. There's even a photograph of the wardrobe and the shoes, pair after pair of them, flimsy as tissue paper, barely capable of supporting the weight of their price tags.

It's a strange and horrible world to which they recruit them young. Tots design their own awful bedrooms. 'Six-year-old Iona has a green and cream toile wallpaper, matching curtains and upholstered slipper chair (slipper chair!) and an old French wooden bed. Georgia, almost twelve . . . has a sophisticated tented ceiling. (What's sophisticated about it is left unsaid. The word itself just stamps its own unarguable assertion. It's sophisticated because it's sophisticated.) Olivia, fourteen, relaxes on her "four-poster" achieved mainly with fabric.' It's all there in that last sentence. In *House-and-Garden* Land cloth is never cloth, nor is it even material. It is always fabric. And Olivia, poor thing, is not relaxing. She is posing for the camera on the 'four-poster' with a dog. Appearances suggest that if Fido were to leap onto the 'four-poster' at any time other than when the *House and Garden* photographer was present it would be sent forthwith to the dog shelter. And the moment the snap was taken, of course, the dog ran off in search of things to kill, eat or roll in and so, if she's got any sense, did Olivia.

Otherwise she's doomed to a life in which 'organic textures, flavours and fragrances set the scene for Christmas in a marquee. Coco husks sprinkled underfoot scent the air with chocolate. A bird bath and terracotta planters sprayed with copper act as centrepieces, encircled with bay leaves and cinnamon sticks and holding branches of twisted willow or reeds and dried orange slices.'

It's all there in sumptuous colour photography, the table ware arrayed around the copper-sprayed bird bath and the dried orange slices. The glasses and napery are set just so. No shots of the aftermath, of course, no candid snaps of stacked and sullied crockery, or of the live-in Filipina treasure with the chapped hands bent over the scullery sink, or of Uncle Trevor drunk as a moose in rut. No record either of the conversation that took place around the copper-sprayed bird bath over the cloying fragrance (no smells allowed in paradise) of the crushed coco husks. Imagine that conversation. On second thoughts, don't bother. Spare yourself. The conversation is irrelevant. It didn't happen. For this is lala-land.

Most telling of all, as you flick through the magazine it's impossible, at a glance, to distinguish the text from the ads. Both picture the perfect, the faultless, the moment before things happen, the moment of expectation, of order, of hope, of idealised material lust, of how things should be but aren't. It's porn.

Grammar with teeth

I taught for twenty years. Now I'm doing it again, part time for a month or two. Nothing's changed. I stand in front of classes and I try to interest them in words. I speak of nouns and verbs and how they reflect the world. I praise the power of simplicity. I say that language is thought, that language is what separates us from the beasts, that shoddy language is a crime. I rant and I clown and I sweat but it doesn't seem to do much good. Most pupils just wait for time to pass. They want to be away and doing. I often think I'm wasting my time. I can rely on only one person to be interested and it seems absurd to drive all the way to school in order to interest myself.

Education is a curious business. And today on this heavy summer Sunday I was going to write about it. I wanted to detail the folly of the NCEA and the bankruptcy of educational theory and the misconception of the nature of the child. I would use a lot of abstract nouns. My tone would be earnest and adult. But then the puppy arrived. I had agreed to look after it for the day. The puppy put paid to earnest and adult.

When people buy a puppy they see it as a bundle of adjectives.

That snub little muzzle is cute. That tottering run is endearing. Those big brown eyes are adorable. But the buyer soon discovers that the adjectives are only a sales pitch. A puppy isn't adjectives. A puppy's a verb. It does stuff. And it learns by doing stuff. For a puppy, to be and to do and to learn are the same verb.

I looked after the puppy for eight hours. During those eight hours it stopped being a verb for approximately five minutes. Those five minutes happened to coincide with the five minutes that I was being a verb. I was restraining the puppy.

A puppy is crammed with vitality. Inside its tiny frame I could feel the verbs squirming. Restraining it was like trying to hold a bag of corks under water.

Abstract nouns don't interest a puppy. Nouns such as education or language or thought are no good because they can't be bitten. What a puppy wants are concrete nouns and this puppy found concrete nouns all over my house. And having found them it bit them in order to learn what they would do.

The shoe didn't do a lot but it tasted faintly of cow. Cow is meat. Meat is food. The puppy chewed the shoe until I got up from the computer and did a verb, whereupon the puppy transferred its attention to another concrete noun. This noun is twelve years old and called Jessie. Jessie is experienced in the ways of puppies. She's a good teacher. The puppy nipped her. Jessie growled. The puppy stood back a moment to absorb the lesson and then decided not to. It nipped her again. Jessie snapped the air an inch from the puppy's nose. This time the puppy absorbed the lesson. But the lesson it absorbed was specific rather than general. The puppy learned not to bite this particular concrete noun. But it didn't learn not to bite all concrete nouns of the same class.

Another concrete noun of the same class was lying on the sofa. His name is Baz. Baz is not experienced in the ways of puppies. He is three years old, 35 kilos, as fit as an orchestra of fiddles and a great killer of possums. The puppy was roughly the size of a possum.

The puppy leapt onto the sofa and bit Baz's ear. Baz did nothing. The puppy bit his cheek. Baz tried to shake the puppy off. The puppy held on. Baz sighed and got off the sofa with the puppy hanging from his cheek like a toothed pendant. I have known several teachers like Baz.

Baz lay down. The puppy was delighted. It discovered a world of prepositions. It walked around Baz and burrowed under him and jumped onto him and clambered over him and bit into him.

To distract the puppy and to rescue Baz I led them into the garden and turned on the hose. The puppy let go of Baz in order to bite the stream of water. But the water acted more like a verb than a noun. It refused to stay bitten. The hose proved a far more satisfactory noun. And then the puppy saw the chooks. Here was food on the move. Here were nouns that did stuff. Suddenly there were verbs everywhere: run, chase, scatter, bark, squawk, fly. I contributed a few verbs myself. Bellow was the first of them, followed by pursue, lunge, miss, slip, fall and swear. The puppy loved it.

And so it went on. The cat was met and barked at. A milk carton was chased and seized and thrown and chased again. And whenever things grew dull there was always Baz to assault. The puppy met a multitude of nouns and committed a multitude of verbs. It learned a lot and it was happier than any kid in school. And all without a word. It was an education.

Pap

I thought for a moment I'd found hope. In the paper last Thursday, just above the story of the sixty-three-year-old Pole who went to hospital complaining of headaches, there was a story about the Queen.

The Queen was hosting a reception for representatives of the British music industry. If I'd been the Queen I'd have pretended to have a headache and joined the Pole in hospital, but the Queen is a better woman than I am. She stayed at home and did her horrible duty. And there's a picture of her doing it.

She is immediately recognisable. She is wearing a standard-issue Queen dress the colour of seasickness. The hemline stands where it has always stood on the Queen, which is there, right there, and not an eighth of an inch either way. The hair, too, is as it's always been, a sort of lacquered motor bike helmet, grey with years of meeting representatives of music industries, but still recognisably the Queen's hair.

Ranged before the Queen are three famous men. There's Jimmy Page of Led Zeppelin, Brian May of Queen, and Mr Eric Clapton. They are standing in attitudes of deference and Mr Clapton is delicately shaking hands with the Queen and bowing from the hips. Despite their fame, however, none of these men is immediately recognisable, for each is wearing a suit. They are not known for wearing suits. They made their names wearing the opposite of suits. They wore jeans and young-person clothes, clothes that announced they were ordinary people, like you or me, and not part of the nasty establishment that repressed ordinary people and kept us away from the power and wealth and fame that were rightfully ours.

If thirty years ago you had shown these musicians a snap of themselves dressed like bankers and deferring to royalty, they would have scoffed. They stood in counterpoint to all that stuff.

And throughout those thirty years, while they shinned up the ladder of success in their jeans, the Queen's just carried on carrying on, lacquering her hair, retaining her hemline and shaking deferential hands. It was the musicians who moved away from her unchanging world and now they have come back to it, speaking politely. I find that ironic, but it's not what gave me the sniff of hope.

The musicians have made a lot of music. Some of it is tuneful but all of it is pap. And I resent it. It is not the pappiness that I resent. There has always been and will always be an abundance of pap in the world and resenting it is like resenting oxygen or lust. What I resent is that this pap has slithered into my skull.

I can hum tunes by Eric Clapton. I can recite lyrics by Queen with only minor inaccuracies. I don't want to. I didn't ask any of it in. It has just occupied the air for all forty-seven years of my life, assaulting me from radios and in lifts and while I have waited for people in suits to answer the telephone. Everywhere I've been, that same music has been too. There is no escaping it.

Unless, that is, you're the Queen. For it was words the Queen spoke that gave me my momentary flutter of hope. As Eric Clapton, the erstwhile youngster, bowed his head and clasped her hand and spoke sweet conventional emptinesses, the Queen apparently said to him, to the universally celebrated Mr Clapton, 'And what exactly do you do?'

I wish I'd been there. I'd have cheered. Cheered at the thought that it might just be possible to escape the universal pap, the musical candyfloss, the shallow emotive background to our shallow emotive lives.

But it can't be done. Unless you're a Queen who lives in rarefied abstraction, the pap gets you in the end. It lodges in the skull and wears you down. If it were possible to buy a cranial vacuum cleaner and suck out all the Eric Clapton pap and the Beatles pap and the Elton Bloody John pap and all the inane rest of it that I've absorbed simply by being alive, I'd be down at Betta Electrical before you could say yellow submarine. But it isn't. The stuff will stay in my head till I keel over. And what's especially cruel it that it will probably stay there when the good stuff starts to leak out.

There I'll be, twenty years from now on a sunny Wednesday afternoon, wedged in a floral armchair in the lounge of the Eventide Home for Withered Hacks, and some well-meaning young thing will breeze in all cheery cheery and sit down at the piano and bash out a whole string of those appalling tunes in the hope that we husks will feel a ghost of a sap-rise and will remember when the world was young. And I'll probably sing along. Oh God. There is no hope.

Except that is for the Pole with the headaches. Apparently the doctors found a 12-centimetre knife blade buried in his skull. They removed it without difficulty. The Pole said he'd probably acquired the knife when he came home drunk and fell off a kitchen stool. Nothing wrong with that of course, but I don't believe him. I suspect he was trying to dig the tunes out.

Weather or not

A low foggy morning. Fog had crept into the harbour basin, had swaddled the port in cotton wool.

Some mornings I feel lithe and alive, with teeth, like an eel. But not this morning. This morning I woke with a clogged head, as though the fog had filled it. I had writing to do but the words came heavy and fat and slow.

I drank coffee of course, and from my best mug, one decorated with the cover design of a novel by Evelyn Waugh. Waugh wrote prose as sharp and as clean and as murderous as a scalpel, but my prose refused to clear.

So I went up the hill with the dogs, through air that was summer-warm and graveyard-still and dense with fog. Fog. Even the word sounds clogged with itself, choked.

Fog's a staple of horror movies. Fog always shrouds the castle of the blood-sucking count, and it smothers the river valley where the murderer lurks, because fog makes a known world mysterious.

We can never know what's round the corner, but when fog descends we don't even know if there's a corner. Fog intensifies our ignorance. The world shrinks to here and very close to here. Fog underlines the present tense. Everything else is unknowable.

But what's round the corner still fascinates us and there have always been people to exploit that fascination. First came the woman with the crystal ball and the talk of tall dark strangers, but these days she has any number of rivals vying to corner the future market: zodiac interpreters, tarot touts, quivering mediums, ouija fraudsters and financial advisers, all of them offering to give us a glimpse of the yet-to-come and all of them every bit as befogged as the client.

And then there are the television weather forecasters. Poor things, they've become celebrities, but it's their own fault.

Like any fairground huckster they now start with a tease, popping into the bulletin early on and promising to give us the low-down on who's going to get wet tomorrow and who's going to bask. It's a titillatory bait no different from the fortune teller's come-on line. It's the promise of a sneak preview of the unknown, an insider tip.

Then when they do appear they drag it out. They tell us first what we already know, presenting the weather that's just gone as a form of competition. Today's prize for the highest temperature goes to plucky little Hororata, and Hororata puffs out its chest and endures the insincere applause of the rest of country.

But then comes the meaty stuff, the future. And thanks to the potent engines of science, the satellites, the monitoring stations, the anemometers in Antarctica, they generally get the short-range forecast right. But unlike science they offer it with judgement attached. Rain gets a grim black symbol on the weather map and the presenter puts on the long face of regret. Whereas sunshine gets a merry symbol and a smile-drenched promise that tomorrow will be a lovely day for a picnic on the Port Hills or some other improbable activity drawn from the *Weather Forecasters Bumper Book of Nice Family Fun*.

In other words the weather forecast appears to be information but in fact it's just a show. A show that tames the unknown. And a show that rests on false assumptions.

The first is the assumption that it is good to know the future. It isn't. Every character in mythology who was granted the gift of foresight ended up in tears.

The second is that we need to know what the weather will be like. Most of us don't. Unless we farm or put to sea in little boats, the weather has little influence over what we do.

The third is that there is good weather and bad weather, kind stuff and cruel. Not so. There is only weather. Without its variety we would all be dead.

And then there is the assumption that we don't like to be surprised. We do like to be surprised. Without surprise there is only boredom.

And so it was this morning, as I lumbered up the hill through the cloud with a head to match. For suddenly, in the space of perhaps 10 yards, I climbed out of the fog and into the summer sun. I stopped and turned and looked. Below me lay a basin of fog, obscuring the town and the port and the water. The fog was a thick-ridged creaminess, like a meringue, seemingly dense enough to walk on. And out of the far side of the fog, the hills of the peninsula rose sharp as cut paper and washed with lemon light.

This is all right, I thought, and I stood to stare, sensing my mind clear as I did so. I came down the hill smiling and keen to work. And if I'd known it was going to be like that it wouldn't have been as good.

Gumdigger

'Pass the Luxator,' said the dentist, and I heard the hygienist open a drawer and rootle through what sounded like a tangle of cutlery.

I didn't see the Luxator because it passed from hygienist to dentist in that area behind the dental chair where worryingly invisible things go on, but I knew what it was going to do. It was going to pull a tooth from my head.

Time was when tooth-pulling was the only sort of dentistry. In the thirteenth century the dentist was the local barber. If, while he was placing the pudding bowl over a customer's scalp in order to deliver the fashionable cut of the day, the customer mentioned that one of his teeth was troubling him, the barber would summon his hygienist. The medieval hygienist was not a young woman with breasts, but rather a grown man with forearms. The barber seized the tooth with forceps while the hygienist seized the patient with determination. The barber pulled, the patient screamed and the hygienist held on.

The only advantage of medieval dentistry was that in the course of your life, even if you suffered from the worst teeth imaginable, you could only go to the dentist thirty-two times. Thereafter you got your haircuts from the gum specialist.

Since then, life and dentistry have evolved in step with each other. In the thirteenth century both were brief, cheap and painful. Today, by and large, they're both long, expensive and painless.

The only other time I've had a tooth out, the dentist was eighty years old and the tooth about eight. This time both dentist and tooth were in their forties. The tooth was an iceberg, nine-tenths of it hidden below the gum line. Above the gum there was only a battered stump, a stump that had been drilled and shaped and pinned and filled I don't know how many times. Each one of those fillings had been a source of pride and income to the dentist who created it, and a source of tutting and income to the dentist who later replaced it.

But now the tooth was beyond salvage, and the dentist and I had had a mature professional discussion about it along the following lines:

Dentist: I think that tooth should go.

Me: Will you have to use the drill?

Dentist: No.

Me: Will it hurt?

Dentist: No.

Me: I think that tooth should go too.

He delivered the anaesthetic with a highly amusing needle a couple of yards in length, then we waited for my lower lip to sag and fill with saliva as with certain children in the lower streams whom it was always a joy to teach. To fill the time I said I expected that advances in technology meant that modern dentists rarely got to pull a tooth. He replied that, on the contrary, he pulled several every day, especially when there were foreign ships in port.

'The Poles and the Russians just don't look after their teeth,' he said. 'They're also impervious to pain. Half of them can't be bothered with an anaesthetic. But the Koreans are all wimps.'

So saying he prodded my gum a bit, asked if it hurt, then called for the Luxator. Gripping my jaw almost as firmly as I was gripping the arms of the chair, he set to work. I did not know what the Luxator looked like, nor could I feel what it was up to, but I imagined it as a sort of space-age miniature vacuum cleaner that would suck the tooth from my jawbone before you could say 'Did I tell you about my Korean heritage?'

Perhaps because the stump was so negligible, the vacuum cleaner took a while to suck. But then there came a graunching sound and a disconcertingly triumphant 'That's got it' from the dentist, and after four merry decades my tooth and I parted company.

'I don't suppose you want to see the tooth,' said the dentist.

He supposed wrong. I am a world-ranked coward but I have never been squeamish. Indeed I take a morbid interest in previously unseen bits of the body. Some years ago one of my dogs was hit by a car. After the operation on his shattered femur the vet showed me a shard of bone that he had been unable to fit back in. I took it home as a grisly souvenir.

As it happened, a couple of days later I showed the bone to the recuperating dog. He sniffed at it, then ate it.

I was not tempted to eat my tooth. It was a sorry thing, discoloured with age and abuse. Far more interesting was the blood-streaked Luxator. It had a worn wooden handle and a grey metal shaft. It certainly wasn't a space-age miniature vacuum cleaner. Indeed it looked like a thirteenth-century screwdriver. The dentist was fingering it with every appearance of affection.

And if I hadn't had a mouth full of blood and cotton wool, and if I hadn't been exploring with my tongue the exciting new gap in my mouth that I shall take to the grave, and if I hadn't been thinking 'one down, thirty-one to go', I'd have asked him to throw in a haircut.

Consider the zip

'Strange to be ignorant of the way things work,' wrote dear old dismal Larkin. Larkin was writing about big things like seasons and reproduction but he might as well have been writing about little things. Things like zips.

Consider the zip. I have one in front of me as I write. Nothing strange in that of course. Like most men I normally have a zip in front of me. Indeed I often have several zips in front of me. When dog-walking I wear a vest that consists almost entirely of zips. There's a zip pocket for the leads, another for cigarettes, another for plastic bags in case someone's watching, and yet another for pieces of dried ox liver with which to bribe the dogs. That jacket and I have done thousands of miles and probably a hundred ox livers. It's a fine and fragrant thing.

But that jacket's by no means my sum total of zips. I own bags with zips and cushions with zips and duvet covers with zips and several of those natty little plastic files with zips. For a recent journey I even bought two pairs of those young person trousers that are more zip than trouser. And of course all my conventional trousers, bar one, have a zip. The exception is the trousers that go with my ancient dinner jacket. Those trousers have a button fly. Over a couple of decades of dress-up functions I have discovered that the ease of operating a button fly is inversely proportional to the urgency of the situation.

Indeed I wouldn't be in the least surprised to learn that in 1893 it was a button fly and a situation of urgency that induced Mr Yashid Khaled Kuzorski of New York to invent, perfect and patent the zip fastener. Then all he had to do was to sit back and wait for the world to beat a path to his door. It did and it continues to do so for the zip is a simple, practical and efficient thing. I can even forgive Mr Kuzorski for stamping his initials on his zips.

But the zip in front of me is no longer efficient. It's the zip down the front of my dog-walking vest and this morning I went to do it up and nothing happened. The zip fastener was stuck fast. So I did the sensible thing and tried to force it. No joy.

I extracted the little thingy from the slot and studied it. It seemed fine. The slot did too, so I reunited them and tried again. And again and again and again. In dog training this is known as an extinction burst.

Let's say, for example, that whenever your dog scratches at the door you let the dog in. The dog has learnt that scratching the door opens it. Then one day the dog scratches at the door and you don't let the dog in, perhaps because you are trying to mend a zip. Does the dog rationalise the situation and say, 'Ah well, scratching doesn't work any more, I suppose I'll have to try turning the handle'? No, it scratches the door harder.

Flies do something similar. They headbut closed windows. And even though there's an open window right alongside, they carry on headbutting the closed one until you either open the window or swat the fly. If you open the window, the fly has learnt that head-butting works. If you swat the fly, well, it's beyond learning. And mention of flies takes me back to the zip.

As I say I repeatedly tried to zip the zip but without success. My extinction burst led eventually to extinction and I brought the thing home unzipped and I laid it on my desk and I studied it.

A zip consists of two ranks of teeth and a thing shaped like a goblet. The ranks of teeth feed separately into the mouth of the goblet and then emerge from its base fused. And for the life of me I can't see how. Without the goblet it is impossible to fuse the teeth. I've tried. I've tried jamming them together. I've tried laying them on top of each other and pressing them together. And yet the goblet appears to be nothing more than, well, a goblet. I've studied the thing with a magnifying glass. And what have I learnt? Zip. Or rather I have learnt that I don't understand how zips work and I would never have invented them.

And in the light of that realisation I look around my study. I see paper. I do not know how to make paper. Plastic, ditto; glass, ditto; metal, ditto; a ballpoint pen, ditto; and as for a telephone or a computer or a printer, ditto in excelsis. If a nuclear blast were to demolish civilisation I'd be the guy sitting whimpering amid the rubble with no idea how to start again. Strange to be ignorant of the way things work indeed, strange and helpless. I shall go to my grave in ignorance, and, unlike Mr Kuzorski, I shall go to that grave without ever having had the wit to invent anything. Unless, that is, you count names like Yashid Khaled Kuzorski.

Dead snapper

When I read that Henri Cartier-Bresson, the French photographer, was dead, I thought of Jill.

One summer in the early eighties I shared a second-floor flat with Jill in dismal north-east London. She worked for a publisher. I didn't work for anyone. I was back from abroad with money in my pocket and an electronic typewriter. I was going to write a novel.

Setting the typewriter on a table at the kitchen window was a mistake. These days my writing desk stands hard against a blank cream wall.

The window overlooked a line of backyards. Each was a few square metres surrounded by a tall brick wall. The yard to the left was a miniature jungle, crammed with a hundred shrubs and bushes in ornamental tubs, all so thickly flourishing that there was barely room for the old duck who owned the flat to squeeze between them with her little yellow watering can. Our backyard was bare concrete and a dustbin. The yard to the right was scattered with urban detritus – a tricycle on its side, a dead washing machine, a heap of nameless rubble, an engine.

The flat that gave onto that yard was rented by a Turkish family. I never saw the father. Mother was huge. Her children were sinuous and feral, like wild cats. They had shaved heads and sharp eyes. The games I watched them play were not war games. They were war. They shed blood. The youngest boy was especially vicious. He threw pieces of metal. He bit. He was about six. I watched him with fascination and wrote nothing.

Each evening Jill would ask me how my novel was going. I told her lies. One day she brought me a book. It was the one present she ever gave me. I gave her none but I did try to sleep with her. We'd been to the pub and talked suggestively. The memory is imprecise but, when we got back to the flat, somehow and dexterously she slid away from me and I expect I was relieved.

The book she gave me was called *After the war was over* and it consisted of black and white photographs. I have always preferred black and white to colour. It seems more faithful. These photos showed scenes from all over Europe in the years following the Second World War, snaps of celebration and misery, of ageing prostitutes in the ruins of Dresden, of children playing war games over the rubble that had been a church.

The photographs of one man stood out. When you turned a page you knew instantaneously whether the snap was one of his without having to read the attribution. That man was Henri Cartier-Bresson.

His photos captured not just the moment, but the meaning of the moment. A kiss by Cartier-Bresson was a single kiss between a returning soldier and a girl in a coat, but at the same time it was all kisses, it was the essence of kiss.

Whatever the talentless polo-neck-sweatered poseurs of the art world may say, photography can only ever be journalism, never art. Cartier-Bresson knew this. He called photography 'un truc mécanique' – a mechanical thing. In old age he threw away his camera and went back to brush and pencil.

Nevertheless his photojournalism was as good as it gets. It cut to the heart of things, gave the viewer a little thrill of seeing that yes, this is how it was, then at that moment. The ancient people in the photograph were people like me.

One afternoon when *After the war was over* lay open on the kitchen table beside the silent typewriter, the vicious Turkish child appeared alone in the derelict backyard. He carried a piece of what looked like bread and laid it with atypical care on the pile of rubble, then went back inside. I stared dreamily into the dim London after-noon, half-heartedly trying to think of words to write and writing nothing.

A pigeon as grey as the sky alighted on the tall brick wall. It checked for danger, fluttered down to the rubble, pecked a couple of times at the bread, swallowed it and took off. Twenty feet up it stopped in mid flight and fell through the air as if shot.

The Turkish boy emerged from the flat. He was whooping. In his hands was a short stout fishing rod with a fixed-spool reel. He'd hooked the pigeon.

He tortured it. He'd pay out line and let the pigeon gain altitude and speed, then yank on the rod and turn the bird from an arrow-head to tumbling chaos, all feathers and legs and panic.

I can see the image now as clearly as a Cartier-Bresson photo-graph, though I can't remember how it ended. With death, probably, but I expect I turned away.

I stayed with Jill the whole summer then went abroad again. My novel never happened. The typewriter's in a landfill somewhere. Cartier-Bresson is as dead as the pigeon. The Turkish child is probably in prison. And as for Jill, I haven't seen her for twenty years but I do know she no longer works for a publisher, or at least not directly. She's become a novelist.

I, speechwriter

I, principal speech-writer to the President of the United States of America, do solemnly swear to write a doozy of a speech for President Bush's – and gee, yeah, I'm as astonished as you are – second inauguration.

When coaching the president in the delivery of this speech, I do solemnly swear to try to stop him grinning like a schoolboy at being re-elected, though I am not confident of success. I shall also encourage him to clench his eyebrows during the serious bits of the speech and to stress the important words.

The most important word for him to stress is liberty (*applause*), which I do solemnly swear to use more than thirty times during the speech, partly because it always spurs applause (*applause*) but mainly because everyone approves of it without being able to define it. If I tire of the word liberty (*applause*) I shall substitute the synonym freedom (*applause*), though I shall not use the word synonym because of potential presidential pronunciation problems. Nor for the same reason shall I use the phrase 'potential presidential pronunciation problems'.

I shall exploit standard rhetorical devices such as the triple construction, the aim of which is not to create a reasoned argument, nor yet to pile evidence on evidence, but simply to sound climactic. A quality that the periodic sentence, of which I shall also make use, reserving as it does its principal word or phrase, most commonly the verb, right to the end of the sentence, sometimes at the risk of mangling the syntax and baffling the audience (*bafflement*), shares.

I further pledge to coin illogical extended metaphors, such as 'the fire that America has lit in the minds of men'. Of this fire I shall say that 'it warms those who feel its power; it burns those who fight its progress; and one day this untamed fire of freedom will reach the darkest corners of our world'. But what this selective fire will do when it reaches those darkest corners, I shall not say. I hope it doesn't burn them down as fires tend to do.

In the course of the speech I shall make great use of the abstract noun courage because it is sometimes induces applause (*silence*). But not always. Nevertheless courage combines with freedom (*applause*) to echo 'the land of the free and the home of the brave' and thus arouse patriotic fervour. Patriotic fervour achieves the first aim of an inaugural speech, which is to numb the power of reason.

The same is true of God (*reverential awe*). Therefore I do also solemnly swear to cram the speech with references to God (*reverential awe*). Not only will they induce a feeling of reverential awe but they will also align the president with the war leaders of history, all of whom from Julius Caesar to Osama bin Laden (*opposite of reverential awe*) have used references to God (*reverential awe*) or gods (*puzzlement*) to encourage their troops.

By these means I shall rewrite the truth of the conflict in Iraq. Rather than portraying it as a self-interested act of invasion, my words will make it seem a selfless act of liberation. And I do solemnly swear not to mention the lies about terrorist links and weapons of mass destruction that the president used to justify the self-interested act of invasion. Those lies are now history and I mean to ignore history.

Except, of course, when history is useful, for I intend to quote from the very historical Abraham Lincoln. This quotation will make the president look learned, will link him with an older and wiser president, and will provide me with another chance for a triple construction. It will also allow me to use the word freedom (*applause*) again.

According to old Abe, 'Those who deny freedom to others deserve it not for themselves, and, under the rule of a just god, cannot long retain it.'

But I shall not pursue these words to their logical conclusion because I do solemnly swear it would screw up the speech. For rather a lot of freedom-denying tyrants – Kim Il Jong, Mao Zedong, Joseph Stalin, Saddam Hussein (*opposite of applause*) and many another – have retained power for rather a long time. Indeed the first three on my list all managed to die in office. The only reasonable conclusion to draw is that there is no just God (*reverential shock*). At the same time it appears that the current president has adopted for himself the role of that just God.

Playing God is not a good look for a devout president so I do solemnly swear to leave the Abe-quote dangling. An inaugural speech does not exist to reach logical conclusions. It exists to appeal to the 90 per cent of Americans who believe in God. With any luck it will also blur the distinction between that God, the President of the United States, and American self-interest (*applause*).

After the speech I do solemnly swear to sink a lot of cocktails at each of the nine inauguration balls. And the reference to balls reminds me that it is time for the standard peroration. May God bless you and may he watch over the United States of America a bit more carefully than he did on the 11th of September 2001 despite constant reminders from every inaugural speech since 1776 that this was his number one priority (*thunderous and sustained applause*).

DNAisy

Francis Crick has died. Fifty years ago Mr Crick solved the riddle of DNA. I'll admit that to me DNA remains a riddle but Mr Crick can hardly be blamed for that.

His discovery made all manner of things possible. He himself lived long enough to witness the birth of Dolly the cloned sheep, an event that couldn't have happened without his research. He also, as it turned out, lived long enough to witness the premature death of Dolly the cloned sheep, but he can hardly be blamed for that, either.

According to a learned article that I read this morning and of which I understood several entire sentences, we share 99 per cent of our DNA with chimpanzees. This nugget of truth is yet another one in the eye for theology. For if, as the theologians have insisted for a couple of thousand years, God made man in his own image, those same theologians are now going to have to acknowledge that the chimp is a pretty faithful self-portrait of the creator as well. Of course the theologians are going to acknowledge no such thing. They've been weaselling their way around all sorts of inconvenient facts for a long time now. They weaselled round Copernicus. They weaselled round Darwin.

In order to weasel round the truth of DNA the whiskered theologians will just shake a crabby finger, say 'ah but', and focus attention on the 1 per cent of DNA that we don't happen to share with our tree-swinging relatives. That 1 per cent, they'll say, is the divine spark. That 1 per cent makes all the difference. They're wrong about the divine spark, but they're right about the difference.

That 1 per cent must contain the blueprint for all the things that we do but chimps don't, everything from motor racing, power point presentations, celebrity chefs, *NZIdol*, pornography, computer games, corporate English, All Black advertising, Ken and Barbie, rhythmic gymnastics, bank fees and dehumidifiers to the wholesale slaughter of daisies. It's a busy bit of DNA.

I mention daisies only because the author of the learned article also mentioned them. He noted in passing that we human beings, in addition to being virtual chimps, also happen to share more than 30 per cent of our DNA with daisies. In other words, up to about thigh level, you and I are plants.

The name daisy derives originally from 'day's eye' because daisies have the endearing habit of closing their petals at night like eyelashes and opening them again in the morning. Perhaps for this reason, the daisy has long been a symbol of humility and innocence.

The reward for this humility and innocence has been persecution. Despite being non-venomous, passive and pretty, daisies are vilified by the suburban gardener for daring to disrupt the uniformity of his lawns. To wage his campaign against them the gardener has a potting shed that resembles a storage room at the Pentagon. It's crammed to the roof beam with weaponry, some of it straightforward hardware like dibbers and trowels, but much of it chemical. What the gardener is engaged in is a holy war, a jihad.

For gardening is a religious belief of which the principal dogma is that some plants are good and others evil. The good ones are called things like *Anagalypta tremens* and cost a lot at the garden centre. The bad ones are called weeds and cost nothing. I can't say it makes a lot of sense to me, but then sense is perhaps too much to expect when one recalls that gardeners, like the rest of us, share 99 per cent of their DNA with gibbering chimps.

But this DNA business stretches beyond both gardeners and theologians. It stretches indeed to that most fashionable of entities, the environment.

We are supposed to care for the environment. We don't. For a start we are all as judgemental as gardeners. As any DOC official will tell you it is easy to raise money to save the waddling kakapo, but less easy to raise money to save the giant worm-eating snail of Taranaki. In other words, we like only the fluffy bits. Our care is sentimental.

It is also selfish. No one, for example, gives a fig about Greenland. But then a shock item on the news tells us the place is melting and everyone starts giving figs by the barrowload. We're scared that Cathedral Square is suddenly going to disappear under 6 feet of water, at which point of course the cathedral will be crammed with theologians saying that this is God's vengeance for our sinfulness and expecting a celestial lifeboat to splash down at any moment in Worcester Street in order to rescue the righteous.

But the whole point is that there is no such thing as the environment as something external that we should care for. The daisies, the kakapo, the snails, the chimps and you and me share vast chunks of DNA. There is no gulf between us. We're it and it's us.

Of course this has always been perfectly obvious from the

beginning. The very fact that we will all croak is evidence enough. But that has never convinced us of our kinship to everything around us. Copernicus couldn't manage it. Nor could Darwin. And Mr Crick, for all the irrefutability of his science, didn't manage it either. We insist on thinking we're special. The 1 per cent difference between us and chimps is invincible vanity.

Let's boulder

When you're frolicking on the hills with a song on your lips and a pair of dogs, and you see a bloke lugging something big up a track, it's only natural to stop and say hello and to ask what the thing is. I stopped and I said hello but I didn't do much asking because the thing was obviously an easel in a case. The man was planning to climb to a scenic niche and then daub something pretty for the tourists or for his own satisfaction or for both. Nevertheless etiquette required me, I thought, to point at the easel case and say 'What's that?', so that the bloke could have the pleasure of telling me with calculated modesty that he was, oh dear, an artist and he was going up the hill to do sensitive creative things and please would I feel both envy and admiration.

And then perhaps I might offer to carry his brushes or smock and together we would climb to a panoramic eminence where I would stand behind him with feigned reverence and genuine curiosity while he laid the first tentative smears of acrylic. And because I had time on my hands, and because I looked forward to privately not thinking much of his painting, and because the dogs would relish another hour sniffing through the undergrowth for something to kill. I pointed at the easel case and said, 'What's that?'

'A bouldering mat.'

'Oh,' I said. Then because that seemed a little unforthcoming, I added, 'What's it for?'

'Bouldering.'

'Oh,' I said. 'Can I watch?' and off we went up the hill together, him carrying his mat and me carrying nothing but enough curiosity to kill a medium-sized cattery.

We climbed to the disused quarry. A hundred years ago they blasted and hacked great cubes of sharp volcanic stuff out of there, but now a grass as fine and soft as maidenhair has carpeted the quarry floor, and scrubby bush has masked the scattering of rocks. The port is out of sight and earshot and the place is windless. It's like a tank of vegetative silence. I've often sat there long and long and thought the place was mine alone. But clearly the boulderers had found it too.

The man led me through the scrub and then he stopped at the quarry wall and laid his mat at the foot of a rock the size of a garage door. Its face was as smooth as a girl's. He shed his jacket, then round his waist he slung a pouch like a Renaissance purse. I asked what it was for.

'Weightlifter's chalk,' he said. He took off his tramping boots and socks and replaced them with a pair of blunt-nosed ballet shoes made from rubber. 'The same stuff they make Formula One tyres out of,' he said.

Bouldering seemed to need a lot of stuff. I don't like stuff. I would, for example, be more likely to go skiing if it didn't require so much stuff: boots, skis, poles, goggles, hat, gloves, ski-pass, four-wheel drive, artificial sun tan, and all for a bit of sliding. These days I am content with a snowless hill and two dogs.

The boulderer sat on his bouldering mat at the base of the rock. He chalked his hands and gripped two tiny ripples in the rock. He nestled one rubber toe into a crevice as deep as a wrinkle on a Labrador's forehead, wedged the other against a protrusion the size of a nipple, and hauled himself up. Though a mere foot or two off the ground he was clinging to the vertical face like a spider on a bedroom wall. He went on to climb the smoothness with deft, deliberate skill, wriggling each toe and finger separately into its niche before shifting his weight onto it.

'It's not about climbing as such,' he said as he climbed. 'It's about setting challenges and overcoming them. It's about technique. It's huge.'

A minute later he was standing on the summit of the boulder. If I'd stretched I could have touched his toes. The boulder's face was dusted with the chalky traces of its conqueror's fingers.

I asked him if he ever fell. 'Sometimes,' he said as he climbed back down. 'That's what the mat's for. But you don't get injured bouldering. Not like mountaineering. Mountaineering's how I broke my back.'

'Oh,' I said, and then 'I see', and thanked him and left. But I wasn't sure that I did see. And as I called the dogs from their forest of smells and went mundanely down the hill on foot, a host of notions flooded through my head. Notions of pointlessness and purpose. Notions of the primitive need to conquer and how at heart we hate the barren sterile safety of the urban twenty-first century and have to engineer synthetic thrills. But then I remembered a night a quarter of a century ago when I climbed to the roof of a parish church and stood in moonlight whooping to the dark and silent village down below. But then again, at the time I thought I was in love.

Dear College of Cardinals

To: CollofCards@Vatican.com
    CC: All World Leaders

Subject: Job Application

Dear College of Cardinals,

Forgive the email but I gather I've got to be quick. Besides, I don't trust the post. The only Italian postman I ever knew was not what one would call conscientious, being only too ready on a warm day to hear the call of the grappa and dump his sack in the Tiber.

Anyway, I'll come straight to the point. I want to be Pope.

I'm sure you're up to here with applications for the job, but before you toss this one into the furnace under St Peter's – and the heating system, by the way, is one of the first things I'd get fixed, by fiat if necessary (though not, for obvious reasons, by Fiat) – I'd just like to point out what makes my application different.

I haven't included a mug shot. That's because I'm flexible. I'm white, of course, but if, as the rumour goes, you're looking for a black bloke this time round, then I'm quite prepared to make with the Nugget. Nor will you catch me complaining that choosing a black bloke because he's black is every bit as racist as not choosing a black bloke because he's black. No, I'm happy to go along with whatever you say. I just want the job and will do what's necessary.

I'm not bothered about salary. So long as there's something dropping into a Vatican Bank Accumulator account every month, I'm not going to haggle about how many zeroes are dangling on the end of it. I realise too that there won't be any pension provision, this not being a job from which you retire, though if you want to throw in a termination clause on the grounds of senility, a gaga get-out as I believe it's known, then that's fine by me. In other words, you dictate the terms and I'll just sign on the dotted. Getting the picture now? I want this job.

Don't worry that I'm an unknown. Who'd heard of old John Paul when he was ministering to the vodka-sodden round the back of Warsaw Cathedral, eh? Precisely. As you and I know, fame comes with the job. And I want it. I like idolatry. Not that I'd call it idolatry, of course, that being fairly strictly verboten in your church (or rather, our church, if you see sense) but I was greatly struck by the recent funeral, queues visible from space, people coming down the steps towards the waxwork papa clamping a hankie to the eyes with one hand and toting a camera-phone above their heads with the other. That's good for business, my friends. It's the sort of stuff I intend to foster not only post-mortem, but pre. Performance popery will be my catch-cry. We're talking celebrity. John Paul set the ball rolling. I'll give it a bloody great shove. You'll love it. I'll have them signing up all over the globe. I'll cram the pews.

The theology I'll leave to you. Just tell me which bits of the Bible we're going to take literally and which bits we're going to deem metaphorical in order to avoid their nasty implications, and I'll do the rest. But could I suggest a pretty staunch unwavering style. Not too many u-turns on the basics. You know, birth control, abortion, creation, female clergy, homosexuality, all the old chestnuts. It's just that the main competition these days are those blokes in the desert, much given to fanaticism, and the only way to compete with fundamental stuff like that is to offer equally fundamental stuff. It gives the punters a life raft to cling to amid the shifting seas of tolerance and liberalism. Everyone pretends to want tolerance etc. but it requires work. What they really want is a set of rules, and then they can just get back to watching six thousand channels of scabrous trash from the great couch of indolence, secure in the knowledge that all the moral issues have been resolved once and for all by the representatives of him upstairs, in other words us.

Not having seen the books, I can't give you a detailed business plan, but I can tell you that I'll be shaking things up a bit. You lot have always been good at real estate, and that sale of indulgences stuff you used to do was a wheeze which might be worth another look, but otherwise, frankly, you're hopeless. I mean, how much did you get for the TV rights to the funeral? Exactly.

My model will be one of the Super 12 rugby franchises down this way, the Crusaders to be precise. (What a pity that title's been taken.) I'll exploit all available methods of marketing to build up a fan base: TV promos, collector cards, stirring music (that's something you've got a head start on) and so on. I want to see 'Don't cross the Papa' plastered across the back bumper of every clapped-out Volvo in Christendom.

What we need, you see, is unswerving loyalty to the cause, because you don't have to be Thomas Aquinas to see which way the global geese are flying. There's a showdown looming. East meets

West. Islam meets Christianity. It'll be just like the glory days of a thousand or so years ago. And when it comes to a showdown, wishy-washy secularism just doesn't cut the mustard. What's needed is dogma plus a figurehead, someone the punters revere and believe in. And that, my clothy friends, should be me. Be bold.

I look forward to hearing from you.

In hope

Joe.

Entropic cookery

S tew's a breeze.

The first thing you need is cheap meat. Get a lot of it and cut it up. But be sure to avoid offal. The Scots get it right. With an accuracy that is frankly atypical, they pronounce offal the same way as they pronounce awful.

The school I attended regularly served liver for lunch. It came in curling slices the colour of asphalt and it landed on your plate with a small but perceptible bounce. Only one child regularly ate it. His name was Doxton. Doxton also ate pens and, if you offered him cash, flies.

The school's reason for serving liver was that it was cheap. The school's excuse for serving liver was that it was good for children. Liver contained iron. So did the hinges on our desks. Admittedly Doxton never suffered anaemia. But he did suffer ostracism.

Anyway, apart from offal, all meat is fine for a stew. The same is more or less true of vegetables. Just steer clear of the green ones. They are the horticultural equivalent of liver. Otherwise pretty well any vegetables that came out on the ground will do. (If they grew above ground keep them for dessert. Only don't call it dessert.

Goulash is followed by dessert. Stew is followed by pudding. The difference between stew and goulash is pretension. The difference between pudding and dessert is size.)

The quality and age of the vegetables are immaterial. Onions with a crown of shoots, carrots you can knot, mushrooms with skin like old people's hands – all these are dandy. Just cut them up. If you want to use fancy vegetables like yams, or zucchini (are these green?), or aubergines the size and shape of a bull's testicles, go ahead. They may make a difference. I wouldn't know. But the base rule of stew is that cheapest is best.

Except for the onions, don't peel the vegetables. Their skin is nutritious. And peeling a potato expends more energy than is left in the potato. Whether you wipe the dirt from the potato before chopping it is a matter of personal taste.

How you chop the vegetables up doesn't matter either, except with the carrots. Never dice carrots. Diced carrots are depression on a plate. They taste of institutions where the uniform has buckles at the back.

So, you've got a pile of meat bits and a pile of vegetable bits. Well done. You're almost there. Now fetch a crock pot. A crock pot is like the offspring of Jesus and a tortoise. It works miracles but slowly.

Bung the meat and vegetables into the crock pot. Tip in some water but not much. Meat and vegetables seem to produce their own water. Don't ask me how. Whatever you do, don't add wine, beer, port, brandy or anything else that's better drunk. Drink it. Booze in the stew doesn't make the stew taste nicer. Booze in the cook does.

Now is the time for the creative bit, the sort of activity that makes television chefs rich. Add stuff. The stuff you add is in your cupboard. It's the stuff you bought packets of when you got sucked in by a television chef. Or else it was left behind by the niece who came to stay and thanked you by cooking tajine of Mongolian lamb with coriander and cumin on the last night instead of going to the pub.

Put in lots of everything. Mixed herbs, tomato sauce, curry powder, chilli powder, gravy browning, bay leaves, anything, in short, that's in the food cupboard but that isn't actually food. Stock powder is good. It doesn't matter what kind. If you've got several kinds, use them all. The correct quantity to add of everything is as much as you like. Few of the things will make any difference. But do include flour. It turns the stew into something that labels on cans of soup call hearty. This means it has the texture of wallpaper paste.

Then the fun part. Put the lid on the crock pot and go away. If, when you come back, nothing has happened, you haven't been away long enough. Or else you haven't turned the crock pot on. If the former, go away again. If the latter, turn it on, then go away again.

How long should you stay away? Well, one day's good, two days are better. The aim of the exercise is entropy. If you can still recognise the ingredients, the stew isn't stew. It's soup. Soup's good but stew's excellent. A stew is a fusion, a melding, a mess, a pottage. A pottage takes time.

Prepare to serve the stew by drinking. Then drink some more. If you've got guests turn the stew into a casserole. This is done by ladling it into a posh dish. To turn it into goulash you can add red stuff. Tomato paste works well. Or else give the guests even more to drink then just tell them it's goulash.

But the best way to eat stew is alone with a dog. Dole the stuff onto two plates and offer the dog a race. The dog will win but that's good for your humility. And the dog will ask for seconds, which is good for your pride. And if you've drunk enough and eaten the stew fast enough, you won't taste it.

Keep 'em poor

Make poverty history, scream the ageing rock stars. Are they out of their minds?

Well, of course they're out of their minds. They're ageing rock stars. Their minds were addled in adolescence by adulation and acid, and re-addled in middle age by knighthoods. But that barely excuses the banality of their thinking. Making poverty history would be disastrous.

Who'd manufacture my underpants, my training shoes, my dehumidifier or the combined key-fob, penlight and nail clipper that I picked up for a song at The Warehouse the other day and that has afforded me such delight? No, sharing out the global goodies sounds all nice and sugary, but when underpants hit the sort of prices that only Tuku Morgan's prepared to pay then the sugar will start to taste rancid. The rich world needs poverty.

Consider golf. At present you can get onto a golfcourse with reasonable ease everywhere but Japan. There may be a bit of a queue on a Sunday morning, but it's no great suffering to hang around in a pair of ghastly Chinese slacks and polo shirt, toying with your Indian-made Pings amid surroundings rendered pleasant by the sort of people who can't afford to belong to the club. Make poverty history, however, and not only would you have to mow your own fairways but you wouldn't be able to get into the clubhouse for the pullulating hordes from Delhi and Darfur waving their newly acquired dollars above their heads, yelling for gin and haggling over the bar prices as if it was some sort of Moroccan street market because they hadn't yet had a century or two of swaddled prosperity to teach them manners. No, it's unthinkable, catastrophic in every way.

The tourism industry would shrivel like the before shot in a Viagra ad. I mean, bung a few dollars into the hands of the deprived and however vigorously you flourish your platinum Amex card outside Dar es Salaam railway station, you won't be able to find a porter. The locals are absolutely charming at present of course because we've got the dosh. But toss them a bit of prosperity and see what happens to those welcoming smiles and garlands of flowers at the airport. Precisely. They'd melt faster than the morning mist over a lump of gorilla-infested jungle in Zaire. Furthermore you wouldn't find locals with an Incentive Saver account hanging around in decorative little huts doing picturesque peasanty things with oxen and pre-industrial agricultural machinery for us to point the Nikon at. No, they'd be razing the gorilla-infested jungle and erecting the African equivalent of Fendalton before you could say embryonic real estate industry. And who's going to go on safari to Fendalton?

Not of course that there'd be anything left to go on safari for. The first thing the newly enriched would do would be exactly what we did when we first started squirrelling the stuff away in bank accounts, which was to eliminate all environmental threats to our well-being. Kalashnikov sales would go through the roof and that would be that for tigers, rhinos, snakes and all the rest of the excitingly nasty bits of nature that we haven't got any more but that we're keen for them to keep. That croc-wrestling Aussie, for example, the one with the shorts and the fake enthusiasm and the billion-decibel whisper, would be out of a job overnight. Nothing to lament in his demise, of course, but with him would go an entire industry that exists purely to indulge and amuse us fatsos in the West, to wit the animal porn business featuring regal predators and rather less regal herbivores being hauled down and having their jugulars punctured for us to enjoy in super slow-mo. All gone. David Attenborough on the dole and the Natural History channel showing either static or documentaries about Cruftos, the Amazon poodle show. Curtains too for *National Geographic* magazine, taking with it a whole tradition of sagging African breasts and closet pre-teen pleasure. And that's just the entertainment side of global poverty.

Start thinking resources and you realise the full insanity of the naive proposals of that Irish rocker who's named after a dog-biscuit. Already, as a result of a mere decade selling underpants, socks and All Black regalia to the West, a few million Chinese have started on the long march to Prosperityville and look what's happened to the price of steel. And have you tried to buy a tonne of copper ore recently? Nor have I as it happens, but apparently the stuff's all headed for Shanghai as fast as they can shovel it out of the ground. As for oil, well, there's precious little left as it is, and if every pauper round the globe got his work-callused mitts on a rusting Corolla it would be $500 a barrel within minutes. Not to mention the pollution which it is our job to produce and theirs to endure the consequences of. Though of course the newly rich would refuse to endure the consequences of it any more, and as global warming rendered everything within a thousand miles of the equator uninhabitable, where would they all be heading next, eh? To war, that's where.

So what are the rockers on about? It's tempting to imagine that it's all a ruse to induce the Third World to forsake its awful traditional music and buy some even more awful rock music. But the rock stars can't be that clever, surely.

Fifty thousand an hour, money-makingly

'O Harry,' said Hermione introductorily, 'I've got this cracking idea for a new plot.

'Good,' said Harry Potter. 'About time.'

'Why do you say that?' asked Hermione interrogatively.

'Well,' said Harry, 'according to the text I'm only fourteen, but in real time I'm in my early twenties and after all those scrapes we've been through together, Hermione, I've got to know you really well and, frankly, my wand . . .'

'O Harry,' interrupted Hermione blush-sparingly, 'you silly beast. Asexuality's a convention of children's literature and so you're going to have to wait till after the final book in the series which probably won't arrive for another year or two. Do you think you can hold on?'

'I'll try,' said Harry leg-crossingly.

'Meanwhile,' said Hermione subject-changingly, 'we need a new plot. Some of the critics have been giving us a bad time. They say the books are clunkily written . . .'

'What?' interrupted Harry clunkily. 'What do they mean, clunkily?'

'And,' continued Hermione apparently non-Harry-hearingly, 'that the whole of our story is simply a corny battle between good and evil using time-worn cliché-ridden medieval imagery.'

As she spoke a silvery-blue dragon reared coincidentally onto its hind legs, writhing with all its might and spitting fire from its vicious-looking fanged mouth, the sparks raining down on its scaly hide.

'Is that all?' asked Harry.

'By no means,' said Hermione. 'They also say that Hogwarts is parodic nostalgia, a sort of Billy Bunter with magic, and that most of the incidental characters speak like Spitfire pilots in black and white films.'

'Whoa, there,' shouted a moustachioed wizard illustratively as he struggled to restrain the dragon on a stout leather leash, 'just look at her plume of fire. Isn't she a beauty?'

'So what do you say to that, Harry?' asked Hermione point-makingly.

'Fifty thousand copies an hour,' said Harry, 'is what I say to that. We're selling fifty thousand copies an hour. The critics are just . . . are just . . . help me out, Hermione.'

'Green with envy,' said Hermione outhelpingly.

'Precisely,' said Harry. 'They're just green with envy. But what's your new plot element?'

'Well,' said Hermione well, 'I think we need a new evil charac-ter, so I've come up with a German.'

'Oh, now that *is* a good idea,' said Harry. 'That fits in nicely with our air of fifties style Britishness. But what's this character's name? Names are everything in our business. We've got Voldemort, who translates, though no one seems to notice, as "flight of death", we've

208

got the posh romanticism of Hermione, the deliberate irony of the ordinariness of Potter, allied to the royal hint in Harry, the Anglo-Saxon consonantality of Hagrid with its intimations of witchcraft, the straightforward demonology of Griffindor, the black and predatory connotations of Ravenclaw, the comic inversion of Warthogs, the . . .'

'Ratzinger,' said Hermione papally.

'Crikey,' said Harry, 'that's good and nasty. Tell me more.'

'As I see it,' said Hermione, 'Ratzinger sings to rats. He's got a cellar full of rats and he sings instructions to them whereupon they rush out on murderous errands. It's great colour stuff, all German and efficient and sinister.'

'I like it,' said Harry.

'But at the same time Ratzinger belongs to a worldwide organisation led by a frail old man who suddenly ups and dies. All the club elders then go into a huddle and choose Ratzinger to take over. They announce their decision by sending smoke out of a chimney.'

'That's a bit far-fetched, isn't it?' said Harry. 'Do you think people will swallow it?'

'You bet,' said Hermione wageringly. 'But the best bit's still to come. Ratzinger changes his name to something nice and puts on all this medieval finery and then, guess what.'

'What?' said Harry.

'He denounces us. Effectively he declares war on Hogwarts. He says that the stories of our adventures are "subtle seductions".'

'Subtle!' exclaimed Harry. 'There's nothing subtle about Harry Potter.'

'Ah but,' butted Hermione, 'the whole point is that he's a competitor. His organisation runs doctrinal schools like ours and deals like us with imaginary forces to which it gives powerful names, and it sets great store by ritual incantations, and it dresses up a lot of its pronouncements in a dead language that only insiders can understand, and it reveres a book of ancient pronouncements, many of which, it must be said, are contradictory, but still it's a powerful force, and though the organisation doesn't officially believe in witches and wizards it nevertheless condemns them as dabblers in the occult which it also officially doesn't believe in, though it did once, and . . .'

'It sounds,' said Harry, 'a pretty mixed-up outfit.'

'But a powerful one,' said Hermione.

'Fifty thousand copies an hour powerful?' asked Harry.

'Of course not,' said Hermione, 'and that's the point. It would love to be fifty thousand copies an hour powerful which is why Ratzinger's having a go at us.'

'Green with envy, then,' said Harry. 'Like all the rest of them.'

A short stack with Ben

I'm in Queenstown but my head's in Idaho. I'm thinking of Ben and the boss-eyed woman and the miserable men. I haven't thought of them for twenty years. The pancakes brought them back.

I'm in a diner. Diners are as American as Cadillacs, but you rarely see them outside America because they are good things. America exports only its bad things. It exports fast food, fat tourists and filthy foreign policy. It exports situation comedies that are as funny as leukaemia. It exports Hollywood fantasies to fuel the dreams of the poor in spirit. It exports television evangelists with wigs and grins. It exports fad diets, theories of management, self-help books and rap. And it wonders why there are parts of the world that despise it.

Until I went there I despised America. When I went there I found more kind and generous people than I had met anywhere else. And I found diners. Every diner had a long counter with stools, and booths along the wall. The moment you sat down you got a glass of iced water and a cup of thin coffee.

The glory of diners was the breakfasts. Steak and eggs, hash browns and sausages, and bacon cooked till it snapped. All was cheap and swift and bountiful and served on plates the size of Wisconsin. I always had the pancakes. They came with whipped butter and a synthetic syrup that they called maple. I would smear ounces of butter between the pancakes, drench the lot in syrup, then carve triple-decker wedges of sopping rich sweetness.

And here, this morning, in Queenstown, I ordered pancakes once again. The syrup smelt authentically inauthentic. And the taste brought with it a gust of memory so strong it almost blew me from my stool.

New Year's Eve 1983 and I awoke in Salt Lake City, Utah, the weird heart of the Mormon world. I had wandered its streets for a couple of days, gawping. But Utah was no place to celebrate New Year's Eve and I hitched north out of town. It took all day to reach Idaho. In the first town beyond the border I dumped my bag at a motel and went in search of New Year's Eve debauch. The town was called, if memory serves, Something Falls. The first shop window I passed had a display of T-shirts. The most prominent said 'Something Falls, Idaho, is not the end of the world, but you can see it from here'.

The town had two bars. One was shut. The other was Herman's Tavern. Next door to Herman's Tavern was Herman's Diner.

In the tavern I found Ben the barman, a boss-eyed woman and a table of miserable men. The men wore check shirts and cat hats and sat in silence.

Ben poured me a beer and asked me what I was doing in Something Falls. I said I was looking for fun on New Year's Eve. When I spoke, the table of miserable men swung slowly round en masse and stared at me as cattle do, their eyes all wide and wondering.

'You sure came to the wrong place,' said Ben.

But it was too late to find another place. I spent that New Year's Eve in Herman's Tavern. I drank pitchers of beer with the miserable men. We barely spoke. I played pool against the boss-eyed woman. One eye aimed north-west, the other south-east. She wore jeans of a size that would be unsellable in any other country. When she bent over the table her backside was like two sacks of cement. She thrashed me.

At midnight, bells rang on the radio. No one reacted. Ten minutes later Ben said, 'Happy New Year, everyone.' I said, 'Happy New Year, Ben.' One of the miserable men said, 'Fuck off, Ben.'

A little later I got up to leave. The same miserable man asked me where I was going. 'To bed,' I said. 'Like hell you are,' he said and he drove me in his pick-up truck to a house and we drank more beer in silence.

In the morning the only place open for breakfast was Herman's Diner. The boss-eyed woman was cooking. Ben was stretched out on the counter asleep. I sat two place settings beyond his feet. His brown leather boots had a hole in the sole. I ordered pancakes from the boss-eyed woman, ate them, paid, then hitched out of Something Falls. I've not been back.

But now the taste of pancakes has taken me back, back to a single frail travelling coincidence, an event of no significance. And it seems to me now that for twenty-six years my life was destined briefly to collide with the lives of Ben and the men and the boss-eyed woman, like a railway line leading inexorably to a junction. The junction came. We met. And then it was over. That was that. I left Something Falls and the lines of our lives sped away from each other. It meant nothing and it means nothing. It just was.

Where are they now? Dead or alive? Still moping in Herman's Tavern? Still soaking up Budweiser and playing pool? I'll never know. I don't want to know.

And yet it pleases me to think of them, to wonder once again at the web of chance. And here, now, in a diner on the other side of the world, I find myself smiling with the mild intoxication of the utterly random. It's as sweet as syrup.

Light thickens with dogs

'Light thickens,' said Macbeth one evening. He did a nice line in poetry even when he was about to commit murder. 'Light thickens, and the crow makes wing to the rooky wood. Good things of day begin to droop and drowse,' and so saying he pulled on his boots and headed off into the night to kill a king.

I don't know what Macbeth was like at walking in the dark. If he was anything like me, he was hopeless. If he was anything like my dogs, he was brilliant.

Darkness doesn't seem to trouble dogs. Perhaps it's because they see in black and white, so shades of grey for them are business as usual. And anyway their noses act like eyes.

Our noses don't. We are visual creatures so darkness disables us, which is why, like Macbeth, we associate day with good and night with evil.

Last night, when all the good things of Lyttelton had long since drooped and drowsed or gone to the pub, I drove the dogs to the bays. When I opened the car door, the dogs bounded into the bush as if it were noon. Both dogs are black. They disappeared. They went with the sure-footedness of goats.

I followed with the sure-footedness of a drunk. Though I know these paths well, I stumbled and slipped, and where the bush was dense I went with a hand outstretched before me as if trying to stop traffic.

In compensation for my blindness my other senses grew acute. A pine tree smelt of disinfectant. A branch brushed my arm and my skin reacted as if electrocuted. And I had ears as sharp as Spock's. For a while I tracked the dogs by sound – a twig snapping, the heavy panting of my younger dog – but then the dogs rounded a corner or dropped over a bluff and I was alone.

> How weak and little is the light,
> All the universe of sight,
> Love and delight,
> Before the might,
> If you love it not, of night.

In town the night has never bothered me. I will amble down the darkest of dark alleys, whistling like a boulevardier in springtime, not caring a fig for the knife-toting ruffians with which any film director would people such a spot. But put me in the wilderness at night, however mild that wilderness might be, and I'm on edge. They say it takes imagination to be scared. If so, then I'm an imaginative man.

I remember as a child walking down a country lane at night and flushing a pheasant. It screeched and rose from right beneath my feet as if fired from a silo. I have often noticed that when a startled bird takes off it spontaneously empties its bowels. When this pheasant took off, so did I.

And I remember taking a party of schoolboys fishing. We camped among trees by the Tekapo River. The fishing was good and when dusk fell I was a mile or two upstream. The trout rose with the moon to suck the day's spent insects from the surface of the pool. The fish were audible. The water shivered like mercury. But the darkness made me clumsy and I caught nothing. Then the fish sank back down and all was silvery and still. As I started the trek back to camp, the stones of the riverbank graunched underfoot. Nameless creatures made moan in the bush.

Moonlight is romantic for a couple, but for this solitary fisherman it felt eerie. I would have liked to sing but didn't dare.

Then in the distance I heard my name called. The kids, who were sixteen years old and urban like me, had long since returned to camp and were concerned that I had not. I called back but I was calling against the breeze. I didn't call again.

It took an hour to walk back. When I reached the camp I met an image as old as mankind. The kids were sitting hunched around a fire, the flames casting giant shifting shadows on the wall of trees. I stepped into the clearing and said 'Hello.' The boys rose like pheasants.

Last night was moonless. On the hillside above me a possum cackled. It's a sound that makes you doubt the beast is vegetarian. Where the scrub had been cleared the grass was thick with frost. It felt and sounded like walking on cornflakes.

On the far side of the water a car's headlights swept around a hillside. Behind it the hills were humped grey silhouettes against the rich ink of the sky. I walked a while then called the dogs. My voice sounded absurdly loud.

My dogs are part-time obedient. I called again. Nothing stirred but the echo of the two short syllables. I became aware of my own breathing.

The cold seeped through the soles of my sandshoes. I thought I would retrace my steps to round a bluff and call again. I turned, stepped out and fell smack over a dog. She had slipped quietly up behind me and had stood there with the patience of nature, waiting for me to acknowledge her, black in the blackness and quite at ease, unable to understand my blindness.

My other dog came panting up the hill. 'Hell is murky,' I said, in echo of Lady Macbeth, and we headed for the lights of home.

For we are young and free

In the same week as the premier of New South Wales has taken steps to encourage Australian patriotism, Shane Warne, the well-known Australian cricketer, has agreed to take part in an episode of *Neighbours*, the well-known Australian drivel. What writer could resist the opportunity to submit a script for the show? Here's mine:

Establishing scene: a beach in the typically Australian town of Girt-by-Sea where typically Australian things are going on. Bush tucker is simmering in a billy on the Harvey Norman barbecue. A mass brawl on the beach is degenerating into a game of Aussie Rules. Surfers pass by en route to Paradise. They ignore a man in a safari suit shouting at crocodiles with bogus enthusiasm. At the high-tide mark, a Lebanese man lies groaning, a 40-ounce bottle of Bundaberg protruding at a decorative angle from his skull. Wholesome Australian girls in bikinis are using him as a beach volleyball net.

Cut to the inside of Matilda's condominium on Billabong Avenue. The doorbell rings. Matilda leaves off frying an emu's egg and waltzes to the door.

Shane Warne is standing on the step. His hair is gelled like a hedge-hog. He is holding a toboggan in one hand and a CD case in the other. Matilda waltzes two steps backwards with surprise, and one sideways.

Shane: Australians all, let us rejoice, for we are young and free.

Matilda: Mr Warne, what a lovely surprise. Been sledging, I see. But what brings you to the set of *Neighbours* where something dramatic happens in every episode, normally illustrating a point of contemporary concern such as racial tension or abortion or Aids, played for cheap emotion by a cast of young people who have been chosen for their sexiness rather than any ability to act?

Shane: Are you Matilda, headmistress of Girt-by-Sea Primary School?

Matilda: That's me, Mr Warne.

Shane: Well, in my capacity as Toohey's Light Patriotism Ambassador for the state of New South Wales, I bring you this. (*He hands her a CD in a green and gold case, etched with an exquisite image of original Australians in traditional tribal costume queuing at a liquor store.*) It's a recording of the national anthem which, by order of the state premier, you are to play at every Girt-by-Sea school assembly from now on, preferably with the children standing and singing along in joyful strains with one hand over their hearts and the other not up their noses.

Matilda: Crikey Dick, Mr Warne, our land may abound in nature's gifts of beauty rich and rare, such as red-back spiders, cane toads and chlamydia-riddled koalas, but don't you think we're getting a

220

bit too much like the America of the South Pacific? Half our armed forces are in Iraq, we're becoming obese, we erect trade barriers on spurious grounds, and we export increasing numbers of tourists who have to shout to be heard above their clothes. So isn't a daily pledge of allegiance in schools just another step down Imitation-Yankee Avenue? Are you trying to come the raw prawn with me, Mr Warne, or some other equally incomprehensible local idiom?

Shane: How's that?

Matilda: Not out, but look who's coming.

Enter several pairs of speedos and miniature bikinis occupied by young Australian neighbours, leading a life of perpetual sunshine and complex coupling arrangements in order to titillate a global audience living in Speedo-and-bikini-less climes.

Shane stops a boy with blue hair.

Shane: What's your name, son?

Boy: Reddy.

Shane: Well, Reddy, are you a proud young Australian?

Reddy: Fair dinkum, Shane.

Shane: Good boy. And are you aware that, according to the premier of New South Wales, 'the national anthem is about community spirit, being a proud Australian and recognising our shared national identity'? And are you furthermore aware that from now on your schooling will include units on 'Australian Values'? And are you even furtherermore aware that our noble premier has defined these Australian values as family values, community harmony, national identity and other deeply meaningful abstract nouns? We've golden soil and wealth for toil and . . .

Matilda: Sorry to interrupt, Mr Warne – and I do deeply admire your efforts in the recent Ashes series, so tragically lost despite your venomous leg-breaks – but isn't this brain-washing? Isn't it the sort of platitudinous blather used throughout the ages to bolster the people in power, to induce uncritical allegiance, and ultimately to turn the young into potential war-fodder?

Shane: No.

Matilda: That's okay then. Right, kids, all together now, 'In joyful strains then let us sing' . . . oh no, look, a bush fire. We're all going to die. Run for it, young Australians, but don't stop singing.

Cut to credits, and nauseating theme music etc.

See me saw

There are tools, there are men's tools, and then there are chain-saws. A chainsaw is carnage on a stick. Whoever thought of the title *The Texas Chainsaw Massacre* could have stopped there. There was no need to make the film. Anyone could picture the pictures.

My neighbour is a manly man. He's got a chainsaw and I have coveted it. I have coveted it so hard I couldn't sleep. I watched him fell a tree last week. Brrrm, brrrm, yeeaow, crack, shudder, topple, BOOM. I find it hard to imagine a more manly sentence than that.

Having chopped the tree down the neighbour then chopped it up. Some time in the future the bits will turn into smoke and heat. Heat for nothing. I wanted free heat too.

My previous house had a gas fire. The gas came in chemistry-lab cylinders at $70 a pop which I didn't mind paying because I had no alternative. But my new house came with a log burner and I resented paying for wood. Wood is everywhere. The stuff grows on trees. I took to collecting driftwood from the beach and twigs from dog walks. But in the evening as I huddled round my twig heap I imagined my neighbour standing like an eighteenth-century squire with his back to a monstrous hearth, spreading his tailcoat to toast his buttocks, and I felt envy.

The solution to envy lay in the steep paddock behind my house where several trees had been felled and forgotten by the previous owner. Those trees were heat for the taking, heat for nothing.

Of the two assistants in the chainsaw shop, one was old and one young. When I stepped through the door they both recognised my manliness on the instant and raced to be first to make its acquaintance. The younger won at a canter.

'I want a chainsaw,' I said, because that's how manly men talk. Terse, spare, emphatic.

'Good,' he said.

'Yes,' I said.

'What size?' he said.

'Big,' I said.

'Right,' he said and he rubbed his hands together in the universal sawyer's gesture indicating free warmth to come.

The chainsaw cost $1800. Protective chaps cost $200, steel-tipped boots $100, safety glasses $25, safety helmet $25 and banana-coloured ear muffs $20. The assistant also wanted to charge me $10 for a petrol can but I raised a manly eyebrow and he threw the can in for free. Most men just shop, you see, but manly men cut deals.

The chainsaw had a 25-inch bar. I liked that. Imperial measurements are manly. When I got the thing home the dogs barked at it. 'Good dogs,' I said, and donned my safety gear.

If you've ever carried a big chainsaw up a steep paddock wearing steel-tipped boots, helmet, glasses, ear muffs, a manly expression and a pair of chaps that seem to be made out of carpet, you'll know that it's warm work. You may also know that it's warm work walking back down a steep paddock to fetch the instruction manual.

The manual kicked off with forty-eight pages of safety instructions all of which I skipped apart from an amusing paragraph about the perils of white finger. Then page forty-nine explained that starting the engine was a simple business of depressing the compression valve, engaging the chain brake, squeezing the throttle trigger, adjusting the cotter pin spindle, calibrating the carburettor sprocket, then setting a steel-tipped toe into the handle of the chainsaw and tweaking the starter rope. And sure enough the mighty beast roared into life before you could say 'two pauses to demist the safety glasses and a mental note to self to ring the chiropractor'.

Stripping a trunk of branches proved entertaining. The chainsaw tended to seek out branches I wasn't aiming at. Then it would leap and roar like a stallion. 'Whoa,' I'd bellow in a manly voice, hoping that the neighbour would emerge to admire me. He didn't but it didn't matter. After little more than an hour I had stripped two yards of trunk. After that it was like slicing a giant salami. The engine roared, sawdust flew and a round dropped, neat as a hockey puck. I cut eight rounds then stilled the engine, laid the saw aside and just stood there, dripping sweat, sprayed with sawdust, my steel-tipped boots planted firmly on my own soil as the sun sank in the west. At my feet a pile of logs. In my heart a primitive satisfaction. I kicked a log. It rolled, gathered momentum, bounced like a tennis ball, cleared the fence, astonished a dog and crashed into the tin wall of the woodshed. The boom echoed round the valley and I felt good.

The logs lasted the whole evening.

Not if, but when

'It's not if,' said a virologist, 'but when.' With that one simple sentence he condemned a nation to its fate. He strapped New Zealand to the railway track as the H5N1 Express bore down en route from Media to Public. The train had no brakes. The track had no points. The metal wheels had no pity. The result was horrible to behold. New Zealand suffered an appalling case of fear of bird flu.

Symptoms vary. According to phobologists, the most obvious sign that the disease has taken hold is a slight but measurable distension of the vocabulary. The words 'virus', 'mutate' and especially 'pandemic' stream from the victim's mouth, along with entire phrases such as 'cross the species barrier'. Such phrases are known to phobologists as 'lexical floaters'. Though they appear to be associated with intellectual substance, closer examination, even under an ordinary household magnifying glass, reveals that they are attached to no scientific knowledge whatsoever.

Phobologists are at pains to remind the public that lexical floaters are extraordinarily contagious and that once contracted they are terminal. Any amateur examination should be conducted in ear muffs.

The fear virus works, say experts, by attaching itself to pre-existing fear radicals, left over from past fear epidemics. Capable of lying dormant for years, these radicals respond instantly to gossip or newspaper articles. They are particularly sensitive to television images, especially if these show scientists in white coats filling test tubes from a multiple glass pipette like a horse comb. Energised by these images, fear radicals will attach themselves automatically to the nearest jargon.

Like all fear viruses, the fear-of-bird-flu virus also contains a memory-killer gene. It supplants and suppresses all memories of fear of SARS, Ebola, Y2K, fat, global warming, tsunami, crime, coffee, cholesterol, earthquakes, paedophilia, the sun, snakes, house price collapse, asteroids, terrorism, rising sea level, butter, spitting, dogs and tap water.

At the same time the virus attacks the part of the brain responsible for reasoning. The skill of drawing conclusions from historical evidence is entirely disabled. Without it the brain cannot discern that previous fears have come to nothing, or that fear of the unknown is usually worse than the unknown when it finally makes itself known.

The effects are immediate. Stockpiling is a common response, as is a sense that the human being is a doomed beast in a hostile world. This can lead to lassitude, depression and fatalism, or to a frantic burst of activity characterised by bunker building or even credit-card binging.

The most extreme symptom appears comical at first but requires immediate hospitalisation. Belief in and prayer to a supreme being who is benign and yet simultaneously responsible for bird flu, is so severe a case of mental inconsistency that it must be treated within moments of infection if the patient is to have any hope of recovery.

Leading phobologists are at odds over the efficacy of vaccines against fear of bird fiu. The makers of one popular vaccine acknowledged that they were uncertain whether their product offered anything other than temporary relief. 'But in the midst of a pandemic such as this one,' said a spokesman for Scottish Distilleries, 'surely any relief is better than none. Our vaccine promises at least one evening free from the fear virus before the end of the world arrives the next morning. Ours is also an ideal vaccine to stockpile. It works in the same temporary way against all known fear viruses, and it improves with age.'

Phobologists and government bodies generally prefer a vaccine known as Tammy-CD. Governments have drawn on vast stockpiles of Tammy-CD to immunise front-line workers such as experts and newsreaders. The active agent in Tammy-CD is the upbeat music of Tammy Wynette, the Country and Implant star. Tammy-CD is believed to work by causing the brain to secrete massive quantities of cheap sentiment, thereby depriving the fear virus of attention and causing it to shrivel.

Experts are united, however, in condemning one common form of treatment. 'The serious news item,' said a leading phobologist, 'suggesting that there is no need to panic, that bird flu may well arrive but there's nothing much anyone can do to stop it and certainly no point in worrying about it before it arrives, and that it will probably prove less deadly than the motor cars that we love, is laughable. By denying the need for panic such an item only adds to that panic.' For evidence he directed reporters to a research paper in a recent issue of *Phobology Quarterly*, entitled 'The Pathology of Panic – or the Corporal Jones Syndrome'.

'In short,' he went on, 'it's too late. The fear of bird flu has now escaped into the general population and there is nothing to do but to let it run its course. Eventually it will peak and be replaced by another fear. Or, of course, by bird flu, which would be a relief.'

Joe, you're an angel

Before last weekend I had attended only one surprise party. When the captain of the lowly rugby team I played for turned forty, an old friend took him to the pub. Meanwhile everyone else he'd ever known descended on his house, hid in the basement and turned out the light.

When the birthday boy came home his wife played the fishwife. We heard it all through the floor. Who did he think he was, buggering off to get drunk when they were supposed to be going out to dinner? She let fly with plenty of the words that journalists render with asterisks. It was a superb performance, though, to be frank, it sounded as though she might have done it before. Finally she sent him down to the basement on a spurious errand.

He opened the door, turned on the light and found himself confronted by every face he knew in the world. For a moment he just stared. Then we burst into 'Happy Birthday' and he burst into tears. He was not the sort of man who is easily given to tears. It was a fine moment.

So when last week a friend proposed a surprise party for his wife's birthday I said it was a splendid idea and what time should we all arrive.

'That's up to you,' he said.

'Eh?' I said.

'You see,' he said, 'it's impossible to keep anything from my wife, so I was wondering whether perhaps, Joe, you might be willing, as a favour, and I'll be in your debt for ever, to have the party at, um, well, you know, your place.'

'My place?'

'Your place.'

Time was when the word party beckoned irresistibly. It sang with excitement and whispered of sex.

Sex rarely attended the same parties I did, but that didn't stop it whispering. And even without sex there were the joys of disinhibition and of watching other people fight.

But not any more. At forty-eight I am now so set in my inhibitions that they have become the whole of me. At the same time the whisper of sex and the bellow of booze have been drowned by the siren song of cocoa and an early night.

As for having a party at my place, well, it was unthinkable. I'd have to clean the toilet. I'd have to stay upright to the end with the sort of people who treat parties in the same way as limpets treat rocks. At four in the morning they'd want to moan about their relationships before rummaging through my bathroom for razor blades. And since it wouldn't actually be my party I wouldn't even know the names of the people who were breaking my furniture, missing the toilet bowl, throwing up in my garden, de-alphabetising my books, leaving glasses of dog-ends beneath my chairs, ransacking my booze cabinet late at night in search of something vivid to make cocktails with, sneaking into my spare bedroom and wedging the door shut with my bookshelves in order to have sex without letting me watch, then crashing on my sofa and farting through the night and being there in the morning to eat my bacon, my eggs and my aspirins. It was out of the question.

'Good idea,' I said. 'Let's have the party at my place.'

'Really?' he said.

'Yes, really,' I said.

'Joe,' he said, 'you're an angel.' Which was nice of him but wrong. I wasn't an angel. I didn't want to host the party. But I did want to seem to want to host the party. I wanted to seem like the sort of generous and uninhibited bloke who spontaneously lends his house to other people to hold parties in. If I'd said no I would have showed myself to be mean and cautious and inhibited and selfish.

As Saturday approached I increasingly cursed myself for having agreed to hold the party, which proved only that I was mean and cautious and inhibited and selfish, a catalogue of adjectives to which I had now added dissembling and hypocritical. But it was too late to back out.

On the big night my task was to collect the birthday girl, take her for a walk with my dogs and then drive her back to my house on the pretext that I'd forgotten her present. In the meantime every one of her multiple relatives, friends and colleagues would have hidden in my lounge and turned off the lights.

When we drove up to my house it seemed impressively deserted. If there were cars I couldn't see them. If there were people I couldn't hear them. I sent the birthday girl upstairs to find her present while I turned the car round. I pictured her walking into the darkened room, turning on the light and screaming.

The scream came bang on cue. By the time I got upstairs she was sipping brandy and merely crying. 'You bastard,' she said when she saw me, which was flattering.

It proved a very middle-aged party. Nothing got broken, everyone thanked me, and by one in the morning they'd all gone home to cocoa. Hubby then spent the next day scrubbing my house to a cleanliness it had never before achieved, and telling me what a top-notch chap I was. And now, three days later, I almost believe I'm the sort of bloke he thinks I am.

Funny and true

What a coup for cartooning. I have heard it suggested that a dozen cartoons, from Denmark of all places, may yet spark World War III. They won't, of course, because the leaders of Islam know they haven't got enough guns, but it's nice to know that the art of caricature still packs a kick.

The purpose of a cartoon is not to be funny. Being funny is the method. The purpose of a cartoon is to tell the truth. Truth is immediately recognisable and often funny.

The Muslim world has not found the cartoons funny. The ostensible reason is that Islam forbids pictures of Mohammed. But that reason doesn't stand up to scrutiny. Five minutes on the Internet and I had discovered several pictures of Mohammed. I am also reliably informed that you can buy a picture of Mohammed in the central market at Teheran. So, there must be something else that's upsetting the Islamic world to the point that they're firebombing embassies, marching down Queen Street and boycotting Danish yoghurt.

I have seen only two of the cartoons. The first depicts Mohammed with a bomb in his turban. It is not particularly witty. The point it is obviously making is that some people commit acts of murder in the name of the prophet. Equally obviously, that point is true.

The reaction of a few Muslims has been funnier than the cartoon. 'Slay those who insult Islam,' said one placard carried by a protester, thereby exquisitely reinforcing the point of the cartoon he is protesting against. He reminds me of the Christian fundamentalist who murdered an abortionist on the grounds that the abortionist committed murder.

The second cartoon is wittier. It depicts Mohammed emerging from Muslim heaven to apologise to a stream of dead suicide bombers for having run out of virgins. The reference is to the promise of 144 virgins to anyone who dies for the Islamic cause. (What attitude this implies to women, I shall ignore for the moment, though it does make me wonder what female suicide bombers get in the hereafter. A gross of Islamic Brad Pitts? A platinum burka?)

What has been ignored amid the eruption of belligerence, apology, and yoghurt-flinging is that the two cartoons invite two simple questions: First, does Islam condone suicide bombers? Does it approve of people blowing themselves up and killing the innocent? If so, then cartoons should be only the start of the mockery. Such a faith should be as universally condemned as Nazism. If not, if Islam does not approve of murder, then every imam and ayatollah should stand up and say so.

Second, is it a tenet of the Islamic faith that suicide bombers get a gross of virgins in heaven? If so, then once again the faith should be universally condemned. If not, then every imam and ayatollah should stand up and say so. And if they did, the hated cartoons would stop.

What has prevented these simple questions being asked is the usual argument about respect. It is our duty, the argument runs, to respect other people's beliefs. I, for one, have never had any idea why. Anything true can always withstand mockery. Copernicus's belief that the earth moved round the sun endured everything the Catholic Inquisition could throw at it. And the Inquisition didn't just print cartoons. It pulled out fingernails. It incinerated its enemies. But the truth endured.

Moreover, the rule about respecting other religions is selectively maintained. If a religion is small it is known as a cult, and a cult is fair game. But the established religions are all former cults. They just happened to get big. Their beliefs are every bit as wacky as the beliefs of little cults. Not questioning those beliefs is not an act of respect. It's merely not upsetting the status quo.

The Western belief that has sparked this controversy is the belief in freedom of speech. It's a belief I share, because history demonstrates that a free press is our best defence against tyranny. Every tyrant in history has muzzled the press.

Ostensibly our leaders share my belief, but when the heat came on they renounced it.

'I approve of freedom of the press,' said Helen Clark on television, 'but . . .'

'I approve of freedom of the press,' said Don Brash on television, 'but . . .'

In other words, both of them worried more about votes or exports than about the truth.

In doing so they echoed Hamdi Hassan, an Egyptian MP. 'Freedom of expression,' said Mr Hassan, 'does not mean people are free to insult prophets.'

236

I'm sorry, Mr Hassan, but that is precisely what it does mean. Freedom means freedom. And if a prophet is really a prophet he's not going to get upset.

The vast majority of the one and a half billion Muslims in this world are good and peaceable people. They don't blow themselves up. They don't hate the West. They are superb hosts. They love their children. They are closer to Mohammed than their leaders are. The same is true of Christians and Christ.

Each religion began with one man. Both men were apparently tolerant. Each man proposed a system of living, a code of social behaviour. After their deaths, however, those teachings became perverted. They became dressed in nonsensical theology. That theology ossified into a system for gaining and retaining power. It became, in other words, merely political. The grip of the Islamic authorities in Iran is indistinguishable from the grip of, say, the Catholic authorities in Spain and Ireland well into the twentieth century, or the grip of the Communist Party in the Soviet Union. Such a grip is a noxious thing.

And if a dozen cartoons can shake it, it's a vulnerable thing.

Dead classy

Class is bad. We sneer at class. We've been taught to. Class is
suppression. Class is just a system for keeping power in the
hands of the few and impotence in the lives of the many. Or so goes
the contemporary wisdom. And, like most contemporary wisdom,
it's far from the whole truth.

Power is always in the hands of the few. If it weren't, it would-
n't be power. The revolutionary expression 'power to the people'
makes as much sense as a speech by Mr Peters. And everyone who
acquires power in the name of the people ends up dead, swinging
by the ankle from a lamppost but still clutching the title deeds to a
fleet of aeroplanes and a holiday home in Antibes with ensuite bul-
lion.

Every society has a system of class. The notion that Soviet Russia
didn't was an obvious myth, as is the notion that New Zealand
doesn't. Just take a walk down the main street now and look. The
system of class is less entrenched here than in some places but it is
emphatically there.

For any system of class to endure it has to be a little squidgy. It
must be possible for a citizen to shift between classes. If the system

238

is squidgeless it becomes ossified and then it shatters. Having shattered, it is always rebuilt. The difference between the old system and the rebuilt one is nugatory.

Class has something to do with money, but it should have something to do with something else. For the word class carries a secondary meaning. If we describe someone as a classy cricketer, it means he plays with an ease and elegance, an apparent disdain for unseemly striving. And so it is with social class. For an upper class to be truly upper it must deport itself in a better way than the masses do. It must take the long view. It must rise above sentiment and simple urges. It must have dignity. It must have, like a duvet, loft. Of course it normally doesn't. True class is rare. But when it does occur, and it can occur anywhere, it's delicious and it's admirable.

Here's a story of class. An old English woman sent it to me recently. She was there. She saw it happen. It was a birthday party.

The old boy whose birthday was being celebrated was turning seventy, three score and ten, the full allotted span beyond which anything is a bonus. He was a distinguished chap in some field or other. His wife was a doctor. She threw the party. She had a surprise present for him. That present was a newly commissioned musical setting of one of Shakespeare's sonnets.

Now, if you're thinking, Oh dear, then I'm with you. I've heard a few musical settings of poetry in my time and I wouldn't want to sit through any of them again. But no one gets everything right.

Of Shakey's 154 sonnets, the undeservedly best known is 'Shall I compare thee to a summer's day?' Mrs Wifely Doctor didn't choose that one. She chose the second best-known and a far better poem. 'When in disgrace with fortune and men's eyes,' it begins, 'I all alone beweep my outcast state.'

She hid a chamber orchestra and a la-di-da tenor behind a curtain before the guests arrived. Then came a couple of hours of eating and drinking and subdued elderly merriment. Eventually a botrytised whatever was served, with coffee and petits fours, the tables were cleared, Mrs Wifely Doctor tapped a spoon against faultless crystal and silence spread like a nice contagion. Birthday Boy stood to speak.

He thanked everyone for coming. He made a little self-abasing joke. And then he faltered. 'I feel a little unwell,' he said. 'I think I'd better sit down.' He smiled a reassuring apology as he spoke, and according to my correspondent he didn't look too bad. Just a bit groggy, she thought, a little woozy with wine and excitement.

He sat down beside his wife on a chair of red plush with ornate gilt mouldings, slumped forward and died. His head hit the table, though without making much of a bang. The hall was silent. Mrs Wifely Doctor felt his pulse. She kissed the top of his head. Then she stood and announced that he was dead and she asked everyone to please stay. She went and came back with four waiters. Under her directions they carried her husband out of the hall on his chair. She returned quite soon.

'This is my present to my husband,' she announced, and the curtain peeled back to reveal the chamber orchestra and the la-di-da tenor who duly delivered the first public performance of an original setting of 'When in disgrace with fortune and men's eyes'.

Now that's class.

Pam's pups

The dictionary defines sentiment as mawkish tenderness. I would define it as the impulse that causes women of a certain age to lean into a pram, say coochy-coo, plant a leathery kiss and give the pram's occupant its first acquaintance with terror.

The subject of sentiment arises because of the events of last weekend. On Saturday morning I discovered that I suddenly had nine extra mouths to feed, and on Sunday morning I discovered Pamela Anderson. Ms Anderson was on the front page of the paper. She was standing between two Royal Canadian Mounted Policemen and behind a similar number of breasts. Each policeman was about the size of an adult fur seal. Each breast was about the size of a fur seal pup.

The comparison is deliberate because Ms Anderson is concerned about fur seal pups. Every year the fishermen of Canada club several thousand fur seal pups to death, and Ms Anderson, along with other luminaries such as Brigitte Bardot and Sir Paul and Lady McCartney, would like to stop them doing so. To this end Ms Anderson has flung the weight of her breasts behind the anti-cull campaign, which should give it significant momentum.

The reason that Ms Anderson is concerned about fur seals cannot be that the species is threatened, because it isn't. The Canadian fur seal population has grown considerably over the last thirty years. No, what Ms Anderson objects to is simply the fact of the innocents being clubbed.

Now, I'm confident Ms Anderson does not object to infant flies being sprayed to death, nor to baby rats being poisoned to death, and I am equally confident that if Ms Anderson were to find a preschooler snake in her bedroom and I were to happen to be passing by and hear her cries of horror and charge heroically into her bedroom and club the thing into the hereafter, Ms Anderson's gratitude would be so all-embracing that I would be threatened with asphyxia. But flies, rats and snakes, of course, are not seal pups. Seal pups have Bambi eyelashes, eyes like saucers and snub little noses. In short they look like human babies. By looking so cute they arouse the soft emotions that mosquito larvae, for example, are utterly incapable of arousing in anyone but Mr and Mrs Mosquito. In other words, Pamela Anderson is being sentimental.

You'll be surprised to learn that I have never clubbed a snake to death in Ms Anderson's bedroom, nor even visited her house, and neither has Ms Anderson visited mine. And I am particularly glad that she didn't pay an inaugural visit a couple of weeks ago because I was doing my best to imitate the Canadian fishermen. I was trying to perform a pre-emptive cull.

I keep chooks. I also keep a rooster. The rooster has achieved a way of life that many men aspire to. He eats, does no work, makes a lot of noise and has sex twenty times a day. Were it not for the sex he could be mistaken for certain members of parliament.

But because of the sex, every egg that is laid on my section is a potential chook. I don't want more chooks and I emphatically don't want more roosters. I try, therefore, to intercept and eat all the eggs, but for obvious evolutionary reasons hens are fond of hiding them. And when a hen of mine disappeared for several days I presumed that she had managed to stash a clutch of eggs and was planning to turn them into a pramful of chooks and roosters. In a bid to thwart her I packed a club and a few essentials in a haversack and set out with the dogs on a search-and-destroy mission. The dogs helpfully dug several hedgehogs out of the undergrowth where they were just settling in for a six-month snooze, but they found no sitting chook, grew bored and gave up. Eventually I did too. 'Good luck to you, chooky,' I said after a fruitless hour of bushwhacking, sat down, opened my haversack, withdrew the essentials and smoked them.

So when the missing chook finally came waddling up over the ridge on Saturday morning, it was with some relief that I noticed she was unaccompanied. Perhaps the rooster had found her ugly. But then out from beneath her peeped a beak, then a body like a fluffy ping-pong ball. It was followed by eight more, all black above and cream below. Ping went my heart, and then pong. I came over, in other words, all Pamela Anderson.

If I had any sense or consistency I would grab the whole brood while they're still catchable, sex them, find homes for the hens and wring the roosters' necks. But I'm no good at sexing chooks until it's obvious, and I'm even less good at neck-wringing. So I am in no position to criticise Pamela Anderson for her sentimental devotion to fur seal pups.

All I can legitimately say is that the sentimental appeal of baby animals is as strong an argument as I know for the truth of the theory of evolution, and that if you're going to be born onto this planet it's a cracking idea to resemble as closely as possible the off-spring of the temporarily dominant species.

Reverend reasoning

Minutes of the AGM of the Intelligent Design Steering Committee, held somewhere on the intelligently designed planet earth.

Attendance: Those attending were the Reverend Peastem, the Very Reverend Drinklittle, the Astonishingly Reverend Archbishop Thimbledick and God.

Apologies: A handwritten apology for absence was received from G.W. Bosh (*sic*) and an apology in Latin from the late Pope (*sick*). Exactly the same apology was received from an unnamed source with the word Pope twinked out and replaced with the words 'Maxim Institute'. A telephone apology was received from The So-Reverend-It-Hurts Bishop Brian Tamaki who said he was there in spirit but was currently too busy ministering to his flock in the diocese of Tithe, Harley and Davidson.

Proceedings: The meeting opened with a prayer to which God listened intently and which he promised to answer just as soon as he'd answered the eight billion others that had landed simultaneously in his in-tray, most of which related to bird flu.

Minutes: The minutes of the previous meeting were read and approved. (*Mover, in a mysterious way: God. Seconder: God.*)

Point of order: The Reverend Peastem queried whether it was constitutionally permissible for the same person to move and second a motion, but God argued through the chair that he was in fact three persons. For evidence he quoted from the Bible, whereupon the chairman congratulated God on the reasoned nature of his argument. 'This is just the sort of deductive scientific method that we on the Intelligent Design Steering Committee seek to promote,' he said.

'Thank you,' said God, and asked for his gratitude to be recorded in the minutes.

'No, we thank you,' said the chairman and moved a motion that the committee thank God for intelligently designing everything. (*Seconder: Thimbledick.*) Peastem proposed that the motion be amended to thank God for intelligently designing 'everything except bird flu, oh, and perhaps leprosy, the Pakistan earthquake, Hurricane Wilma and genital warts' but the amendment did not find a seconder. The unamended motion was passed nem con. (*Abstention: God.*)

General Business: Only one agenda item had been tabled, the bid to have Intelligent Design included in the school science curriculum throughout the Western world. As chairman of the ad hoc subcommittee the Very Reverend Drinklittle reported that the campaign was proving successful because it had been intelligently designed. (*Laughter*) He attributed the momentum of the campaign to three specific causes, the first of which was branding. Changing the name from Creationism to Intelligent Design had completely altered its image in the public mind. It was now seen as a scientific theory rather than as a wishful belief. (*Coughing*) The second principal driver of success was funding. The extraordinary sums contributed by American business interests to support the campaign and also to establish propaganda bodies amusingly known as think-tanks had enabled the campaign to achieve unprecedented market penetration. 'In conclusion,' said the Very Reverend, 'it is the opinion of the ad hoc sub-committee that within ten years the average child will emerge from school unable to distinguish scientific method from a hamburger, and will consider both to be examples of Intelligent Design.' (*Applause, cheers, general acclamation, stamping of feet and an impromptu chorus of 'I'm no kin to the monkey, the monkey's no kin to me' enthusiastically conducted by Thimbledick with the femur of a chimpanzee.*)

The chairman congratulated Drinklittle on his sub-committee's success but reminded him that he had mentioned three contributing causes and wondered whether perhaps he might enlighten the assembly as to the nature of the third. In reply the Very Reverend merely looked towards God, bowed his head and said, 'Thank you.' (*Acclamation, blushes from God etc.*)

'Without your help,' said the Astonishingly Reverend, 'we would never have been able to stem the advancing tide of thought. Branding and money are all very well, but if we hadn't created you in our image, you would never have been able to create us in yours. (*Chorus of 'Great reasoning, Rev', 'Yeeha' and other expressions of religious awe.*) And if we hadn't intelligently designed you so that you could have intelligently designed us, we would never have felt justified in considering ourselves superior to the beasts of the field and the dogs of the kennel, nor would we have felt entitled to eternal life and all the rest of the fringe benefits that come from being your loved and intelligently designed children.

'Thanks to you, our current funding, and a multi-media advertising blitz scheduled for the spring, there is every reason to hope that the devil Darwin and his heretical dependence on observation and repeatable controlled experiments, will be beaten back to the superstitious jungle where it belongs and the Western world can advance on the sort of theocracy that the Middle East has had the good sense to maintain all along. And then we can have a real cracker of a war.'

There being no other business the meeting closed at 8.41 pm with the traditional chorus: 'All things bright and beautiful' sang the happy steering committee,

> *All creatures great and small*
> *All things wise and wonderful*
> *The Lord God intelligently designed them all.*

('Except,' added Peastem *sotto voce*, 'for bird flu, leprosy, the Pakistan earthquake, Hurricane Wilma and genital warts' but such was the general delight that nobody heard him.)

One

There are times when one's outrage boils like an unattended kettle, and now is such a time. There are times when one is obliged to speak up, and now is such a time. And there are times when one has no choice but to use the pronoun one.

'One' is such a magnificently pompous word. It levers itself up onto the stool of self-importance and sneers at the crowd. It brooks no possibility of being wrong. It implies that one represents all people who think right, and that the people who think wrong are insects to be swatted. Let them sneer, as insects are famous for doing, and let them biff their rotten fruit, ditto. When one is unquestionably right, one wears a decoration of rotten fruit as a war hero wears his medals.

The subject about which one wishes to express an opinion today is golf. One has expressed an opinion about golf before. Several years ago one suggested – no, one never suggests – one stated that recreational golf is as obvious an embodiment as one is ever likely to meet of human futility.

The reaction was predictable. One was accused, among other things, of despising golf because one wasn't any good at it.

Naturally one dismissed such reaction with a haughty disregard and a noise best rendered on paper as harrumph, partly because that is the sort of thing one does, but mainly because one's accusers were golfers.

But today one is content to leave the recreational golfers to their folly, and instead one wishes to turn one's magisterial attention to professional golf. This, you will be astonished to hear, is golf played for money, and the first question one must ask is why anyone should pay someone else to play golf. Why, for example, do Volvo sponsor a golf tournament? Do they imagine that by associating themselves with professional golfers, they will sell more of their dreary Swedish cars to recreational golfers? The answer is yes. Furthermore they are bang right, which confirms everything one believes about golfers.

But the feature of the infantile wealth-laden circus of professional golf that has attracted one's magisterial attention is the US Masters – and oh, how that word sings with irony when one considers the people to whom the title is applied, but let that be.

The US Masters, as you may know, is played in Augusta, Georgia, a place of suffocating heat, cotton plantations and black people understandably singing the blues. Until remarkably recently the old boobies who run Augusta maintained the great Southern tradition of racial segregation, until indeed a freak by the name of Tiger Woods became so skilled at the great pointlessness that the boobies felt he was probably entitled to order a drink at their bar rather than just to pour it.

But this is not, as it happens, the point of one's moral outrage today, and neither indeed is Mr Woods, though his name does deserve a brief digression. Does the name Tiger appear on his birth certificate? Did the vicar lean over his crib and intone 'I christen this child Tiger. Long may he put'? One asks only because his name typifies the nonsensical and increasingly common myth-making of sporting nomenclature. In this region of the globe, for example, one notes the preposterously titled Canterbury Crusaders. and even more preposterously in the north of England there exists a rugby league team called the Leeds Rhinos. One can see the points of similarity between rugby league players and myopic pachyderms, but Leeds is hardly the high veldt. Still, let one leave that conundrum hanging in the air like summer cirrus, for one has a more substantial fish in the frying pan.

You will probably have seen Augusta on television, but if you are lucky enough not to have done, you can take it from one that it is faultless. It looks as Eden might have looked if Adam and Eve had had several thousand black servants and a set of Pings. The water features have the deep alluring blue of a Hollywood starlet's contact lenses. The turf is lusher than it has any right to be. The land has been so manicured, pedicured and facialled that it looks synthetic. In short, it's repellent.

The intention is clear. The setting is designed to imply that the beings who strut this course in their vile clothes are the denizens of Arcadia. They are a higher order of being. One is supposed to admire them, and to wish to emulate them. At which thought one feels obliged to emit another harrumph.

But what has really got to one, what has caused one's long-simmering pot of distaste to become a furiously overboiling vat of loathing, was one's discovery that the authorities at Augusta are so serious about the fake image they wish to impart that, and one is not making this up, they dye the water. They dye the water on the golf course so that it looks nice and blue on television. In the face of which fact, to be quite frank, one is lost for words.

Hitch

Late on Friday night, I'm driving north up State Highway One, and somewhere beyond Temuka I see two figures by the road. They appear as silhouettes, young men slouching along the verge, somehow grotesque. They are hitching. I stop. I almost always do. As an ex-hitchhiker I feel obliged. Besides I am intrigued. Few people hitch late at night. I sniff a hint of adventure by proxy, of some sort of drama. Otherwise why should they be here in agricultural nowhere at eleven at night, far from pubs and lights? Also I am tired. I have felt my concentration drifting, my eyelids lowering. I could use some company.

I pull over on gravel 50 metres beyond them and shift a sweater and a burger wrapper from the passenger seat. The lads take a while to reach the car, then one taps hesitantly on the window. They are unsure whether I have stopped for them. A lift this late at night is too much to hope for. I lower the window.

'Where you heading for?'

'Ashburton.'

It's about 70 kilometres to Ashburton. I tell them to get in. They whoop with surprised delight.

One gets in the back, the other in the front. They're both about eighteen.

'Can we smoke?' asks the one in the back.

'Go ahead,' I say, and again they give a little whoop and chuckle. Both roll themselves a cigarette. 'Sweet,' says the one in the back.

'Sweet as,' says his mate.

'Your job,' I say, 'is to keep me awake. Tell me stuff. Tell me stories.'

'Stories?'

'Yeah, anything. Stuff that's happened to you. Just keep talking. You can start with why you're out here hitching.'

The lad in the front has a stainless steel curtain ring hooped through his lip. He tells me they'd driven that morning to Geraldine where they got drunk. They slept off the afternoon somewhere then discovered they'd lost the car keys. They walked the back roads to reach the main road.

'That's some walk,' I say.

The lad shrugs.

'What would have happened if I hadn't stopped for you?'

The lad shrugs again and laughs. 'Whatever,' he says, and I find myself admiring their insouciance. I suspect we all most admire the qualities we lack.

'Go on,' I say, 'tell me stories.'

And the lad in the front seat starts a rambling monologue that takes us all the way to Ashburton. The stories are all concerned with drink and with hating the police and above all with cars. He loves to drive. He lives to drive.

'Get a tank of gas and we just go. Four of us drove to Dunedin once, just for the hell of it. Did most of it at 150 clicks. Then we got a burger and went to Nelson. It was sweet.'

254

He tells me how the cops once followed him from Ashburton to Hinds when he was drunk and his car wasn't registered and he was temporarily without a licence. 'I was bricking it. I hate those bastards.'

In the back seat the other lad is silent. I glance back and he has fallen asleep, his head slumped on his shoulder and juddering against the window. His mate happily carries on, bathing in the stories of his own profligacy and recklessness. He's half boasting, half reminiscing. He tells me how he loves to pick up hitchhikers and terrify them by driving at enormous speed.

'Picked up these two chicks once near Orari and we went on the back roads and got up to 200 clicks and then did a whole load of donuts. They were screaming. Jeez, it was funny.'

I ask if all his friends drive like he does.

'Pretty much,' he says and tells me with wonder in his voice about his friend who's got a 300-horsepower car.

'Have any of your mates died?'

'No,' he says and seems surprised by the question.

His crowning story is semi-coherent. It involves being stopped three times in twelve hours by the police when he was driving an illegal vehicle. The police issued green stickers which, I gather, indicate that the car must not be driven, but he just peeled them off and drove on. He collected, he says, $4000 worth of fines in the one day. He is part proud, and part appalled that his freedom should be so circumscribed.

We reach Ashburton. I ask him where they want to be dropped off and he tells me one block back from the highway. I say I'll drive them to the door and again the lad gives a little whoop of almost childish glee.

'My missus will be up,' he says.

He wakes his mate. I pull up at their gate. They give me directions to get back to the highway and then thank me for the lift with surprising formality.

I watch them shamble up the drive, then I head for home. As I drive sedately through the night I reflect that though their behaviour is inexcusable, stupid, brutish and a lethal threat, I liked them. And a tiny part of me envied them.

Welcome

Dawn. I greet the new day with a cough by Benson and Hedges. I fill and fire the coffee machine, then pad downstairs, a dog at my feet. I am going to fetch the paper. In my fancy new house I pause at the door that grants what is known in real estate circles as internal access to the garage. When I use the term 'real estate circles' I am quoting Dante.

On the far side of the door I hear faint squeaking. I prick my ears. The dog hears it too but doesn't prick his ears because labrador ears don't prick. They just arch slightly at the leading edge, like eyebrows, lending the dog a winsome appearance. I pay no attention to the winsomeness of the dog. I pause, pricked. The dog pauses, floppily intent.

The squeaking is odd, faint, repeated, very high pitched, as if the garage were full of pre-pubescent burglars. I look at the dog. Despite being a labrador he is territorial. He is keen to go. I open the door. Having spent twenty years teaching, there is a part of me that would like to see a territorial labrador among trapped pre-pubescents.

I see no pre-pubescents. I see a black flicker, then another. The dog sees them too. Side by side we stand and look. I have a garage-ful of swallows.

It takes a while to decide exactly how many there are. They dart and glide and dive and swoop, now here, now gone, now under, now over, flipping, arcing, rolling, turning, touching nothing, skirting everything, always squeaking, like bats. They wheel round the lumbering bulk of my car, impossibly precise. It's a big garage. They fill it. There are two of them.

I've seen them before. Last week they came to the garage one evening and they returned again and again to the corner by a high shelf of books that I have stored there because I cannot burn or sell them. Sometimes the swallows would perch on the books, like tiny feathered spearheads, suddenly immobile, faultless. They didn't perch for long. Swallows never seem to perch for long.

Ted Hughes was good on the swallow. He called it 'a whiplash swimmer, a fish of the air'. The swallow was 'the seamstress of summer. She scissors the blue into shapes and she sews it', and the line has the same swing as the flight of the bird.

But swallows aren't seamstresses. They are murderers. That scissoring is feeding. They are catching insects. Only seriously saintly people have sympathy for insects. I don't. Swallows don't. Insects are countless, unpretty, insensate. Swallows are feathered and pretty and closer to us.

I see swallows often when fishing. They whirl and dive and squeak an inch above the water, spearing invisible insects, being swallows. Being swallows is all they do. Simplicity in feathers.

I expect the dog to bark and make a clumsy hopeless charge at the birds. But like me he just stands, following their flight with the great hulk of his head. The swallows seem like a privilege, a blessing, a kindness, a gift, sleek and untroubled. You never see an old swallow. Any failure, any decay, any slip from perfection, any loss of aerobatic deftness, and the swallow can't feed and the swallow dies. But I've never seen a dead one. Swallows inhabit only summers.

My new house is seriously fancy. I press a button and the garage door groans, rumbles and opens. When it is a quarter open, the swallows whip down and through the gap like the flung swings of a fairground ride. They are gone.

Down the zigzag drive I pad with the dog, the half-light sweet with bellbirds. The trees are wet. The air is held promise that the day will dissolve. The paper lies furled on the drive. The dog fetches it in his great soft mouth, his teeth as precise as a swallow's flight. He brings it up to me, his body swinging, writhing with the pleasure of capture. I take the paper. He lets it go gently. Not even a dent in the cellophane from those great white teeth. Many a time I've seen those teeth break a possum's neck. Instantly.

The garage is empty. Up to the kitchen. The coffee machine stands charged and steaming. I pour and sit and unwrap the paper. Newsreader salaries, newsreader squeaking, Hayley Westenra's crush, house prices, spitting, terror of bird flu, Winston Peters. I lay the paper aside, sip the good coffee, light a cigarette, and shut my eyes to see the swallows. I hope they come back. I hope they nest with me.

Flies say no

Seven in the morning and the sun is rumbling over the ridge to toast the creamy flanks of my house and the black flanks of my dogs. It will herd the dogs into the shade and it will haul forth their pink, wet tongues to pulse through the heat of day. And it will quicken the flies. I am at peace with the house and the dogs, but I am at war with the flies. I hate them. I kill them without compunction. I gloat over their corpses. My hatred is pure and good.

The dogs get bones each morning and the flies get the bones for the rest of the day. The flies gather while the dogs are chewing. They circle the dogs, corruption on wings. The noise that the flies carry tingles the hairs in my ears.

The dogs are on my side, on the side of creation. They snap at the flies, teeth clashing with a precise and potent threat. The flies evade the great teeth with mocking ease. They fizz a few inches away, hungry, impatient, eager to corrupt, certain of victory. They will inherit the bones and the earth. They want both now. They are entropy. Black and hairy, shrunken nightmares fashioned into flesh. And what flesh. No meat to them. No honest red muscle. No haunch. Swat a fly and there's only an ooze of stuff, like pus. Pus that draws another fly to perch on its brother with brittle suckered feet, and to feast.

Flies zigzag everywhere. Into corners, seeking residue, remains, decay, the gone and the was. Into my kitchen, revelling in my slovenliness, the crumbs around my toaster, the buttered knife in the sink, the dregs and spills, the offal of living. They worry too at the seal on the fridge, wanting the good, wanting to make it bad. I keep fly swats everywhere, like a paranoid billionaire whose mansion bristles with guns. I am always ready to defend by attacking. I swing wildly, carving the air, enraging the flies. The buzz shifts up through the gears, through the octaves. The rage is good. It drives them full tilt into glass. On glass I can kill. And I do. Three, four, five flailings of the swat, then the tiny grim crunch and sudden silence. The sweetness of death.

I, who am not squeamish, hate to handle the stilled and weightless corpse. I shovel it up with the quivering swat-tip, unload it into the sink, turn on the tap. Gone. But never gone, never while summer lasts. Summer is flies. The unstoppable horde, the flip-side of summer growth, the antonym of good, of love, of yes. Flies say no.

And then, last week, a woman told me of a fly-trap. 'It kills,' she said, 'and it kills good. We get no flies.' I wanted no flies. I sourced the fly trap, drove 15 miles to buy it, brought it home like booty. I assembled it according to the instructions with eager impatient fingers. The flies fizzed around me as I worked, checking out their fate.

A 10-litre paint pail, a hole cut into the lid. Into the paint pail a few inches of water and a heart, a sheep's heart, bought from the butcher for pennies. The heart has to be weighted down beneath the water, to be slowly cooked by the heat of the day, to make soup. For the weight I used the head of a hammer. Then over the hole goes the fly trap, a frisbee of plastic with a vane of sorts on its topside and a well in its centre and holes to release the smell of soup. The same holes let the flies in but not out. Lured by a rotting heart. So apt. So very good.

The trap takes one warm day to mature. That day was yesterday. It caught no flies. But five minutes ago I left the keyboard and my cool basement study and I climbed the stairs into the day's warmth and, with dogs watching incuriously from the shade, I studied my trap. Whoever invented it had read my mind. He made the frisbee transparent so I could see the doomed flies, circling in the pail, drenched, saturated in the smell they love, and quite unable to escape from it, done in by their own desires. Lovely. There were three of them. When darkness comes the pail will cool, the vapour will condense and the flies will tumble from the sheer walls and they will drown, unseen and unlamented.

In time the decomposing flies will supplant the heart as bait. The flies will flock to their own necropolis. I cannot wait.

I went to the kitchen to make a celebratory coffee. A fly fizzed past my scalp, perched on the frying pan. I reached for the swat. The war is never won. But in this house at least there is growth in the armoury of good. We angels fight. We must.

The threshold of the ginge

I wish to propose a toast. On a Tuesday morning in snow-bound Lyttelton I am raising a glass with bubbles in it to the boffins of Louisville University, Kentucky. They are my US Cavalry. They may have arrived forty years too late to do my psyche much good, but I am still grateful. They have confirmed something that I have always known but that no one else has ever believed. I'm sensitive. I feel pain more than you feel pain. Now the boffins have revealed why. I'm sensitive because I'm a red-head.

I'm not a redhead any more. I'm a baldhead with wisps. But those wisps are the remnants of a head of hair that forty years ago was visible from space. It was the bane of my childhood. Goldilocks, they called me, or Ginge or Carrot-top. As a child, if I wanted to hide from my mother at the supermarket I just bur-rowed into a display of oranges.

And I did want to hide from my mother because my mother wanted to take me to the dentist. As far as I recall, most of my childhood consisted of being dragged to the dentist, heels dug in like a recalcitrant puppy, wailing like a world-ranked professional mourner, and smelling faintly of oranges. I wailed and dug because the dentist hurt.

Our family dentist was called Mr Wisher. I wasn't alone in dreading Mr Wisher. He was Victorian and brutal. His drill was operated by a bicycle chain that he wound with his spare hand. The waiting room door had a bolt on it.

But then we shifted to a twentieth-century dentist called Nice Mr Mabberly. Nice Mr Mabberly gave anaesthetics and even asked what flavour you wanted. I always asked for strawberry and didn't mind the injection. But then he drilled and I did mind the drill. I minded because it hurt. 'Tut tut,' said my mother and Nice Mr Mabberly as they peeled me from the ceiling. 'It can't hurt. You've had an injection.' They were wrong. It did hurt. And now forty years on I know why.

'Redheads,' says Louisville University, Kentucky, and I'm quoting, 'need more local anaesthetic at the dentist than the general population.' And that's science. So suck on that, Nice Mr Mabberly. Suck on that, Mother (though I mean that in the kindest possible way).

The reason it hurt, according to the lovely boffins, is that carrot-tops have a special gene. It is Celtic in origin and it dictates that we have 'a lower pain threshold'. Bang right, boffins, and thank you. My pain threshold is subterranean.

At university I took up boxing. I did it mainly to prove to myself that I wasn't the wuss that everyone had told me I was because of my threshold. I impressed the trainer with my walloping of the punch bag and was the first of the novices to be given a bout. I can still remember my opponent. He was an aristo called Rupert. He had mouse-coloured hair. The bell rang and I hit Rupert. I hit him hard and repeatedly. Boxing was lovely and I was good at it. I was mentally lifting the world light-heavyweight crown, the cheque that came with it, and the label of 'wuss' from my shoulders, when Rupert hit me. He hit me on the side of the head and then on the nose and then on the side of the head again. 'Ow,' I said and then 'ow' and then 'ow'. Of course I should have hit Rupert back and I briefly considered doing so but it's difficult to hit someone when you've turned your back on him and covered your head with your hands. It's also hard to take aim when you're crying. I jumped out of the ring, went home and never came back. That night my pillow whispered 'wuss'.

It was the same with rugby. I liked rugby but I couldn't bear to be rucked. 'A little tickle-up with the studs', they called it. I called it excruciating. I would let people know it hurt. 'Wuss,' they said. 'Worse than wuss,' they thought. If only they'd known. If only I'd known.

In cross-country I used to get a stitch. A schoolmate who was good at running told me that the way to deal with a stitch was to keep running until it went away. Ha. Same as if you're stabbed on the way to work the best thing to do is to carry on as normal. When I got a stitch I had no choice but to lie down in the mud like a dying lamb and bleat at the Great Ewe in the sky. 'Oi, Ewe,' I'd bleat, 'why me?'

How easy it would have been for the Great Ewe to tell me about my gene. But no. It took science to do that, as usual. Here's mud in your eye, Kentucky, and thank you.

Rod and gut

I told her I had been away fishing with friends. She snorted.

'That's so . . .' she said, then paused and I saw the muscles at the top of her cheeks tense and bulge as she sought the best word to express her distaste. She found the word. 'It's so primitive,' she said. 'Fishing is just primitive.'

'Mmm,' I said and sipped at my fancy foreign lager. She was drinking the same fancy foreign lager, but had put it aside on the bar so she could reinforce words with gestures. The gestures were not loving gestures, not peaceable gestures.

'There you are, a bunch of sad blokes finding yourselves washed up on the infertile beach of middle age and feeling castrated by a changed world, by the rise of women, by us having seen through you and being no longer obliged to suck up to you and warm your slippers and tolerate your smugness, so off you toddle into the bush in pursuit of fish that you don't need, solely so that you can beat your chests and play King Kong in the theatre of your own mind. It's primitive, regressive, wrong.'

She paused. She wanted a reaction. She wanted me to toss another log on the fire of her disdain.

'Mmm,' I said.

'Is that it?' she said.

'It's the word primitive that puzzles me,' I said. 'If, by primitive, you mean wading into the wide flat of a river early on an autumn evening and standing thigh-deep in the water waiting for the light to fade amid bush, bush that's grown and died and fallen and rotted without purpose for thousands of years, for hundreds of thousands of years, and as the sun's last rays quit the tips of the trees and the night seeps in and a weka screams and a morepork calls from deep in the bush and is answered from somewhere deeper, the mirrored surface of the river flat starts to dimple with the hatching of the caddis flies and those flies infest the air and cling to the brim of your hat and alight on your lips and cheeks and wriggle down the neck of your shirt and the back of your shirt so that you writhe and swat, and what may be an eel knocks against your leg, but then you hear the first splash of a trout rising to those hatching flies and all thoughts of discomfort melt on the instant and you become taut, intent, aware only of fish and water, and the rises become more frequent and are visible in the dark as concentric glinting swirls of steely water and you peel the line from your reel and cast with all the delicacy you can muster and your fly lands invisibly on the black water and in the area where it ought to be you hear a splash and you strike and either the water erupts into hooked fish or it doesn't, if that's what you mean by primitive, then yes, fishing is primitive.'

I took a sip of lager. So did she. Her eyebrows told me to go on, to dig my grave a little deeper. I picked up the spade.

'Or if, by primitive, you mean arriving one morning at the flood plain of a big river, and you stand on the stop bank to scan the water for the dark torpedoes of trout and to assess where it will be possible to cross and where it will be best to fish and what direction the wind is coming from, and the morning is bright with the promise of fishjoy, and you slither down the bank and step into the cold fringe of the river's vastness and feel the sheer weight of the water against your legs, the huge unstoppable tonnage of water pouring off the mountains, hundreds of thousands of tons of it on the constant move, and you are there to raid it, to try to pluck fish from its hugeness, and all that you have to raid it with are your wits, a 10-foot rod, a line that tapers to a nylon point too fine to see, and at its tip a barbed nymph the size of a maggot, so that your venture seems not so much an act of hunting as an act of bravado against monstrous odds, an impertinence, an audacity, and yet against these odds you cast your puny line into a likely flow and the line tip veers to one side and you strike and feel the thrilling chunk of a fish that plunges faster than thought towards deeper water, and your reel screams and your rod bends and you whoop whoop whoop for the fierce joy that has hold of you, if that is what you mean by primitive then you and I look on that word in different ways. You think it bad. I don't.'

And we both sipped at our lager.

Speak to us

Speaking puzzles me.

In private I speak a lot because my dogs find my voice mellifluous, my opinions incisive and my wit uproarious. But I am also sometimes asked to speak in public.

Some people offer me money to speak. Others offer me the pleasure of their company, a cup of tea and an aptly named rock cake.

The occasions that I am asked to speak at often surprise me. One was a fund-raising event at a suburban tennis club. It sounded polite. It turned into an all-in brawl. At the end of the evening furniture was being broken over skulls. On the phone the following morning the tone of the club secretary seemed to imply that I was partly responsible.

On another occasion a rugby league club invited me to address its members. I expected a male audience of a down-to-earth nature. What I did not expect was to be the warm-up act for a strip show. I still believe I should have been informed. Two minutes into my speech the audience became impatient to move on to the next item of the agenda. They expressed that impatience with words and then missiles. I did not stay to watch the performance of my fellow artistes.

Recently, for reasons known only to themselves, I was invited to address a conference of statisticians. I know nothing of statistics. Nevertheless I did not hesitate to point out to them that 73 per cent of statistics were simply invented. Nobody laughed.

I have spoken to groups of the old and groups of the young. I have spoken to a conference of people who operate buses. I have spoken to breakfast clubs and dinner clubs and investing clubs. I once addressed a gathering of stockbrokers (Is there a collective noun for stockbrokers? If not, could I suggest a drear?) and I took the opportunity to explain money to them. The dollar, I said, did not exist. It was merely a shared belief. If people stopped believing in it, the dollar would disappear like a burst balloon. The response of the stockbrokers was less forthright than that of the rugby league players, but it was identical in tone.

I am grateful to my speaking jobs for the money they've earned me, the glimpses they've given me into other people's lives, and the funny stories they've afforded me once the pain has worn off, but I remain puzzled by them.

If I turn down an invitation to speak, the inviter always asks whether I know someone else who can do the job. The implication is obvious. Rather than having sought me out for my unrivalled combination of wit and beauty, they came to me simply because they'd heard that I might be able to plug their gap. That gap is the speaker's gap and what puzzles me is that the speaker's gap exists. Why do people want speakers?

Most speeches are dull. People don't so much enjoy them as endure them. Think of the speeches you have heard at prize givings.

Think of the votes of thanks, the sermons, the Queen at Christmas, the aftermatch formalities, the wedding stuff, the inaugurations, the formal welcomes, the keynote addresses (whatever keynote may mean), the motivational nonsense, the staff meetings.

And yet I know several people who make a living entirely from public speaking. There are bureaux from which you can hire speakers at preposterous expense. A large number of these speakers are known not for their speaking but for something else – for climbing mountains, say, or for playing netball. Playing netball is an admirable thing, as is climbing Mount Cook on one leg without oxygen and with a goat over each shoulder, but neither guarantees a good speech. Presuming that it does is like expecting an All Black to be able to repair the hard drive of your computer on the grounds that he's an All Black.

But there exists something in the psyche of our society that says an event is not an event unless it is consecrated by a speech. I don't know why.

I was once hired to address a school reunion. I had not attended that school. I knew no one at the reunion. I was hired only because the organisers felt that a speaker was needed. He wasn't. Most of the audience had not seen each other for anything up to fifty years. They had plenty to talk about. But the occasion required that they shut up and listen to me. I did not stay on my feet for long.

A while later I went to the urinal. Two elderly men were already there, talking. They didn't notice my arrival.

'That was a great evening,' said one.

'Yeah,' said the other, 'apart from that bastard who spoke.'

'Hear hear,' I said softly to the porcelain, and toddled home with my cheque.

I want some of that

Before July 1980, I'd have said anaphylaxis was a Greek novelist. Then I got stung by a wasp. It almost proved to be the last time I got stung by anything.

The wasp got me on the back of the neck. By the time I reached hospital I looked like the elephant man on one of his worse mornings. My neck was wider than my shoulders. They had to turn me sideways to get me through the door. Breathing was proving an absorbing challenge.

The doctor injected adrenaline directly into my vein. To say it was exciting is like saying that the war in Iraq was misguided. Intravenous adrenaline is almost worth being stung for.

A few years later I met a girl in France whose father was an allergist. He offered me a free course of desensitisation. The process involved injecting me with a minute quantity of wasp venom and then holding me captive in the surgery. Monsieur le Médecin's ostensible purpose was to ensure I didn't suffer an adverse reaction. His actual purpose was to deliver an hour-long illustrated lecture on why England and the English sucked. I never went back. I preferred, on balance, to run the risk of meeting the Greek novelist again.

For the subsequent quarter of a century wasps have left me alone, but I have been reminded of them recently because I am tempted to start keeping bees. I am not allergic to bees.

I don't know very much about beekeeping but I suspect that there's not much keeping involved. If the bees decide to leave I can't see myself shooing them back into the hive. I also doubt the dogs' ability to muster bees. (To be frank I doubt my dogs' ability to muster anything except an appetite, though Jessie used to be a dab hand at shunting chooks around the garden to no purpose.)

I'm not certain what attracts me to beekeeping. It certainly isn't the uniform. I don't see much joy in togging up as if for a moon landing and then clambering up the hill in the middle of the summer carrying a sort of fire extinguisher in order to pacify and rob several thousand armed insects. The reward, of course, comes in the form of honey but for one thing it takes an awful lot of bees an awful lot of time to make not an awful lot of honey, and for another thing I don't like honey. And even if I did I could get a jar of it for five bucks from the supermarket without dressing up like Neil Armstrong.

No, if I kept bees it would be in the same way as I keep dogs, goats, a cat and tadpoles (and whitebait until the cat got them). It would be non-productive, costly indeed (though tadpoles are admittedly inexpensive to feed) and my rewards would be only pleasure and interest. And animals are easier to live with than people.

Since conceiving this interest, I have read a little about bees. They are seriously odd. Everything centres on the queen who is selected young like the Dalai Lama and fattened on royal jelly. She then buzzes out of the hive once, mates and returns to lay eggs. On a good day she can pump out 3000. But she doesn't have to raise the family. All that stuff's done by the workers who are female but infertile. Workers nurse larvae, clean the hive, guard the hive, collect nectar, make honey, make wax, store the honey behind the wax, clean the lavatories and die young.

Bloke bees meanwhile lie back with their heads on their hands, dabbling in poetry, sipping cocktails and once in a while getting up, yawning, stretching, and toddling over to the queen to see if she fancies a bit of rumpety pumpety. It all sounds admirable. It's also ruthless. When the mating season's over so is life for the blokes. They're starved and driven from the hive whereupon they're not going to get taken in out of sympathy by any old drones' home. A short life but a merry one.

But apparently it is wrong to think of bees as individuals. The hive is rather a single organism like a human body and we should think of individual bees in the same way as we think of body parts. So, just as we don't consider kidneys to be independent entities that resent their lousy job and dream of promotion, so we shouldn't fret about individual bees. They are part of the whole, like kidneys, like cells, and the whole is everything. Bees don't mind dying.

All of which I find intriguing and I think I'd like to have some of that around the place, though how you go about starting is something I haven't learned. But I have learned that bees are often attacked and killed by wasps. I think bees and I could get on.

On making a bed

Oh dear, I've been walloped by envy. I want to start again. Because of a bed.

Beds don't matter much. This winter I spent two months overseas and hired a different bed for each of sixty nights. They shared a horizontal quality, more or less, but nothing else. Some sagged. Some were stiff with sheets and blankets, some wildly European with duvets, many rich with evidence of previous occupants detectable by nose and eye, or even touch. But I slept fine in all of them.

I've never bought a bed. My first house came with two. I've slept in one with dogs for eighteen years, and those among my guests who have not cared to join us have occupied the other. They've not complained and nor have I, except in warmer summers, and then it's simply been a case of making with the aerosol and all the fleas have died. Fear and guilt and even what I thought was love have stopped me sleeping, but never once the bed. In short, my bed has served.

But recently the bed has wilted. The thing has lost its buoyancy, the will to boost the dogs and me against the pull of the earth. In winter that's just dandy. It makes a warm and snug cocoon for us to wallow in. But I fear the heat of summer.

And so I went to buy a bed. The bed shop offered beds of every kind except for waterbeds which once were everywhere but suddenly in 1996 or thereabouts they all collectively and simultaneously sprang a leak and shrivelled into landfill. I don't know why.

Nor do I know the collective noun for beds – a slumbrousness, perhaps – but here for me in this enormous showroom it was a bewilderment of beds. So many, so various, and yet so similar.

An assistant sashayed over.

'I want a bed,' I said.

'What sort of bed?' he said.

'A nice one.'

The assistant led me through a string of questions designed to find the bang right bed for me and me alone. Among other things he asked me the position I slept in.

'Lying down,' I said.

'Ha ha,' he said.

'Ha ha,' I said, although I didn't get the joke.

'Show me,' he said, which seemed a little intimate, but I lay on the nearest bed, a sumptuousness of foam and no doubt hidden science, set within a bedroom's worth of chests of drawers with tilting mirrors, bedside tables and a dinky reading light. And there in front of the assistant I curled into the foetal shape that I've adopted every sober night since Kennedy was shot, and closed my eyes.

'Right,' he said. 'I think the bed you need is . . .'

'This one,' I said, for I was bored already and the bed felt fine. 'How much?'

He named a sum.

'No, no,' I said, 'I don't want all the beds in the shop. How much for this bed?'

He repeated the sum.

'Golly,' I said. 'And how much is it without the bedroom's worth of incidental furniture?'

He repeated the sum. 'Golly,' I said, 'but at least the mattress is comfortable.'

'The mattress is extra,' he said.

'Golly,' I said again. When I've found the aptest word I'm not afraid of repetition. 'To sum up, then, for something close to $3000 I get a bed without a mattress.'

'You're onto it,' he said.

I left. I'd made a resolution. I would make a bed. It can't be hard – a frame, some slats, a bolt or two, then slap a mattress on the top and get your head down. I said as much to a friend in the pub, a part-time cabinet-maker. 'It's harder than you think,' he said, 'but if you like I'll make you one.'

'How much?' I said.

The price he named was good. 'A deal,' I said.

He delivered it this morning. The thing's a wonder. It's solid as Mount Cook. The headboard gleams, its ancient heartwood rimu grain a maze of loveliness. The slats are firm as a bank. The whole's as square as Don Brash. I knew as we assembled it that I could never have made it.

And I was seized, racked, filled, crammed, with envy and admiration and regret. Envy of the skill of making. Admiration for the skill of making. And regret that I would never learn to make.

To make is good. Instead of spending time on hateful work to earn the dosh to buy the things we want, we should work less and save the dosh by making. How good and fresh and personal and true to make the furniture you use. How right and satisfying.

I want, right now, to start again, at school, and this time I will work in Harry Barker's woodwork class instead of playing pranks. But that's a dream. Too late, old boy. I'll write these words and take regret to bed.

Mister Muster

Failure is better than success. Failure is funny and it teaches you stuff. It also inoculates you against hubris, the pride that the gods enjoy pumping into your heart before they introduce the banana skin.

In general, then, I am a fan of failure. But today I have to report a success, a success that has pumped me as full as a blimp with hubris. The event was the summer muster.

The summer muster is a staple of televisual farming. It appears on *Country Calendar* and on Speight's ads, which are more or less the same thing. Farmers prepare for the muster by donning Drizabones, applying make-up for that seriously weathered look, mounting horses, surrounding themselves with dogs, and riding slowly up the winding track towards the snowline, saddle-bags crammed with tins of beans and the air thick with guitar music. Then the director shouts cut, the music stops, the farmers dismount, the horses go back to the props department and everyone gets into a Toyota Hilux.

My muster involved neither horses nor Hiluxes. It involved two sheep, two goats, one small paddock and one large labrador. What made it a triumph was that they said it couldn't be done.

By they I mean he. He was a Banks Peninsula farmer with whom I played cricket last week. Actually he was watching the cricket rather than playing, because he had been temporarily disabled. A calf had kicked him in the knee for reasons that the farmer did not elaborate.

I explained my mustering plans to him in the hope of receiving tips. I received discouragement. After ten minutes of discouragement I was tempted to drive to Banks Peninsula and buy the calf a beer.

It was the labrador that provoked the farmer's particular scorn. Labs were, he said, the very worst dogs with sheep. He told me cheerfully how many labs he had had to shoot. They totalled one, but one was ample to alarm me.

I readily admit that Baz is not a sheep dog. He would like to be a sheep dog, I suspect, but only in the manner that a lion would like to be a wildebeest dog.

'Forget it, Joe,' said the farmer in summary. 'Get a proper dog and someone who knows what they're doing.'

I told him that I had got someone who knew what she was doing, a warm-hearted woman who keeps a few sheep, and shears them herself. She is approaching seventy years of age but I didn't tell the farmer that.

Averil arrived at my station on Tuesday morning with two sets of shearing blades and an infectious confidence that I would have liked to be infected by. We climbed to my steep little paddock. Averil admired the pen in the corner, and pretended to admire the race that I had constructed out of waratahs and chicken wire. Baz the lab and I had tested the race that morning by trying to herd the chooks down it. Baz enjoyed the procedure enormously but didn't quite cotton onto its purpose. The chooks cottoned onto it immediately. I consoled myself with the thought that sheep can't fly.

The sheep and goats had taken refuge in a distant corner of the paddock. Averil waited by the race while Baz and I went up the hill to muster. We took with us, respectively, a vigorously wagging tail and a vigorously beating heart.

The sheep stared at the dog. The goats stared at the dog. The dog stared back. 'No,' I said, and he didn't. 'Stay,' I said, and he did. I approached the stock. They skittered down the hill. The dog did not move. 'Good dog,' I said in a tone of voice that I hoped did not betray my astonishment.

'Come,' I said, and he came. 'Sit,' I said, and he sat. The stock skittered further down the hill. I skittered after them. Every few yards I summoned Baz and repositioned him. It was like repeatedly shifting a roadblock with teeth. That the stock moved away from the roadblock did not surprise me. That the roadblock did not move towards the stock, did.

We crept ever closer to the chicken-wire race. The stock made a bid for liberty up the hill. 'Stay,' I said and the roadblock stayed. So did the stock. I held my breath. The stock moved towards the pen. Man, woman and dog closed in. And the goats and the sheep went meekly into the pen. 'Well, bugger me,' I said. The hills were ringing with the gods' applause.

Five minutes later I was learning how to shear and Baz was fast asleep under a pine tree.

Shearing proved a breeze. We whistled through it. When the dog woke up an hour later we were already onto the second sheep.

Another forty minutes and Baz didn't even bother to stand as the goats and the shorn sheep raced past him and out of the pen.

The fleeces were as rich and sweet and dense as pride. I carried them down the hill like booty, my labrador sheep dog happy at my heels, my heart as fat as a cauliflower, my mind already riffling through the phone book in search of a Banks Peninsula number, and my eyes scanning the horizon for the banana skin to come.

The grid of seduction

My mother telephoned at Christmas and I learned that she does Sudoku. My mother is eighty-two.

I do Sudoku as well. I am forty-eight. My dogs don't do Sudoku. My dogs are dogs.

My mother says that she does Sudoku because she enjoys it but also because the exercise of thinking helps to fend off Alzheimer's. I enjoy Sudoku too, but I don't feel the need to fend off Alzheimer's because I smoke. Apparently few smokers go gaga. Either there is something in cigarette smoke that keeps the marbles in place or else cigarettes kill you before the marbles can wander.

I do Sudoku over breakfast while the dogs chew bones. A bone engrosses a dog but a bowl of Hubbard's Yours Fruitfully doesn't engross me. I need brain fodder at the same time. Sudoku is the purest brain fodder. It is ruthlessly logical.

The logical patterns are inflexible. If a, then b, and if b, then c. There is no guesswork. In the harder puzzles the chain of logic extends: if a then b, if b then c, if c then d, and if d, what was a again? For what makes the hard puzzles hard is that they test the limits of the short-term memory, the number of mental balls you can keep simultaneously in the air.

It is similar to telephone numbers. If you tell someone a six-digit number they will be able to recite it back to you. Seven digits and they possibly won't. Nine, and they definitely won't.

Whenever I do a Sudoku puzzle I am reminded of fourth-form algebra. Our teacher was Dim Jim who had eyebrows like caterpillars. His Bible was Hall's *Algebra*. It was a hard-bound book the colour of withered orange-peel and it consisted mainly of columns of exercises. There would be, say, fifty quadratic equations of increasing difficulty. Dim Jim would demonstrate the method required to solve a quadratic, a demonstration that involved much caterpillar activity, then he would set us to work our way down the column of examples while he sat at the desk and gave the caterpillars a break. I liked the whole business. I liked the moment when I grasped how the method worked, I liked applying the method, and I liked the neat way it solved the problem.

No one ever asked Dim Jim what quadratic equations were good for and if they had, Dim Jim would have just waggled the caterpillars a bit and told us to get on with it or else. For quadratics, as far as I can tell, have no purpose. I have never met a quadratic equation since the fourth form and now that more than half my life is over I can confidently predict that I won't. But I can still recall the pleasure of solving them.

They were a perfect, vacuum-sealed world, complete unto itself, where problems had solutions and where when something was done it was done. The rest of school was not like that. It was an indeterminate mess. Hence the pleasure of algebra, which was not a mess, and also of Sudoku. But hence also the addiction.

There is a moment in a Sudoku puzzle when you crack it. Though only half the grid may be complete you know that what lies ahead will be straightforward. Two minutes later the grid is full and that's that.

I read recently that the only phrase Hitler knew in any foreign language was 'Vous êtes mon prisonnier'. That is exactly how I feel when I complete a Sudoku puzzle. It is what I've been striving to achieve for the last half-hour. It ought to be a good moment. But it isn't a good moment. It's a bad moment. What was engrossing throughout a bowl of Yours Fruitfully, a mug of thick coffee and three cigarettes is suddenly dead and devoid of interest. I am post intellectual orgasm.

And just as post actual orgasm I wonder what all the excitement was about and whether the expensive and protracted game was worth the brief flaming of the candle, so it is with Sudoku. My brain is now bereft of a precise and achievable task. I am faced with the mess of the day ahead, the day of inconclusive imprecisions, of shades of grey. Unless, of course, there's another Sudoku puzzle available, its grid temptingly incomplete, offering me the pleasure of its perfect logical sanctuary. I start again on the trudge up the hill to another pointless and disappointing intellectual spasm of relief.

Sudoku is a pastime. It is formulated to please our fat brains. It is adapted to gratify us as the world isn't. My dogs don't need pastimes. They finish their bones and then, if there's nothing going on, they sleep.

Up Apophthegm Mountain

I'm a sucker for the big notion, the sort of thing you find in the *Dictionary of Quotations*. Give me an apophthegm like 'Life can only be understood backwards; but it must be lived forwards' or 'If you want to make God laugh, tell him your plans' and I'll swallow it whole and commit it to memory. For the next few days I'll also regurgitate it whole to anyone who'll listen. And a fat lot of good it does either of us.

For the grand notion never quite fits. It rings true in principle but it omits the detail that constantly muddies the picture, the sort of detail to which I woke this morning. Drizzle masked the hills, my nose was full of snot and I had a hangover that turned my head into the mental equivalent of television static.

I should have spent the morning working but instead I spent it reading the collected letters of a dead and gloom-drenched poet who lived, it seems, in perpetual drizzle. The letters are crammed with small stuff, stuff that mattered at the time but doesn't matter now, stuff like recalcitrant lawnmowers and the price of chops. But then suddenly he startled me with a nugget of big stuff. 'If my life were a week,' he wrote at the age of forty-eight, 'then this would be Friday afternoon.'

The words pierced the hangover and the snot and sank deep into the pink. Ooh, I said, with a delicious shudder of dread, and I laid aside the book.

For I too am forty-eight. I too am on Friday afternoon, and there's only the weekend to go. Oh golly gosh.

As for the week so far, well, all the important stuff happened on Monday, and I've forgotten the lot. It's all gone, all the stuff that dictated every subsequent event has shrivelled into oblivion. When I look back on Monday I see only a vague and sunny land of lala. Tuesday morning was more of the same, but then round about lunchtime up rolled puberty and the weather turned thunderous. There followed an intense afternoon of rich and self-indulgent despair, the air charged with threat and thrill. Nothing since has matched it. Wednesday I spent more or less drunk. Thursday was industrious, energetic and stable. And then came Friday. Friday proved surprising.

Early on Friday I went back to the land where I was born and caught up with old friends from school and university, all of us the same age. And I found myself moving from crisis to crisis. It was as if a switch had been thrown in every male head. Stable Thursday lives had suddenly turned into Friday chaos. Husbands of model diligence had eloped with feather-headed long-legged secretaries. Sensible stockbrokers who slept in ironed pyjamas had fled to the hills to be potters. Everywhere I went, careers were in abeyance and marriages were rubble.

Rather than being a holiday visitor, I became an itinerant counsellor, a shoulder for weeping on, a receptacle for the big questions. I enjoyed every minute of it. And the synchronicity of it fascinated me. It was as if everyone had woken independently to the awareness that this was Friday morning, that the peak of the week had passed and that if a life was ever going to amount to anything it had better start amounting now. It was a subconscious crack of the existential whip.

I saw most of the wayward ones again this year. They'd mostly settled back down. Marriages were patched, careers resumed, and everyone had snuggled down to a Friday afternoon snooze amid the welter of small stuff.

And that in the end is what's wrong with the grand notion. It's all very well to clamber up Apophthegm Mountain to take in the big picture, the tour d'horizon, the great sweep of things, but all too soon it's time to return to the place we belong, down among the small stuff.

All other life forms have the instinctual good sense to stay down there the whole time. You don't see ants wandering off to become painters or to have a final fling before the loins wither into silence. They simply keep on keeping on.

My aged dog has just lain beside my chair. She's twelve years old, which in dog terms is Sunday lunchtime. She neither knows nor cares. Food and hunting and other dogs still interest her, and that will do. The big stuff is a uniquely human interest and it doesn't get us far.

'We are unsuited,' wrote the same gloom-laden poet whose letters I was reading, 'to the long perspectives open at each moment of our lives.' However neat and appealing it may seem, the grand notion, the vision of one's life as a week, is less significant in the end than a hangover, snot, drizzle, a recalcitrant lawnmower or the price of chops.